An Analysis of

Jean-Jacques Rousseau's

The Social Contract

James Hill

Routledge
Taylor & Francis Group

LONDON AND NEW YORK

Published by Macat International Ltd
24:13 Coda Centre, 189 Munster Road, London SW6 6AW.

Distributed exclusively by Routledge
2 Park Square, Milton Park, Abingdon, Oxon OX14 4RN
605 Third Avenue, New York, NY 10017

Routledge is an imprint of the Taylor & Francis Group, an informa business

www.macat.com
info@macat.com

Cataloguing in Publication Data
A catalogue record for this book is available from the British Library.
Library of Congress Cataloguing-in-Publication Data is available upon request.
Cover illustration: Gérard Goffaux

ISBN 978-1-912303-45-8 (hardback)
ISBN 978-1-912127-10-8 (paperback)
ISBN 978-1-912282-33-3 (e-book)

Notice

CONTENTS

THE MACAT LIBRARY

The Macat Library is a series of unique academic explorations of seminal works in the humanities and social sciences – books and papers that have had a significant and widely recognised impact on their disciplines. It has been created to serve as much more than just a summary of what lies between the covers of a great book. It illuminates and explores the influences on, ideas of, and impact of that book. Our goal is to offer a learning resource that encourages critical thinking and fosters a better, deeper understanding of important ideas.

Each publication is divided into three Sections: Influences, Ideas, and Impact. Each Section has four Modules. These explore every important facet of the work, and the responses to it.

This Section-Module structure makes a Macat Library book easy to use, but it has another important feature. Because each Macat book is written to the same format, it is possible (and encouraged!) to cross-reference multiple Macat books along the same lines of inquiry or research. This allows the reader to open up interesting interdisciplinary pathways.

To further aid your reading, lists of glossary terms and people mentioned are included at the end of this book (these are indicated by an asterisk [*] throughout) – as well as a list of works cited.

Macat has worked with the University of Cambridge to identify the elements of critical thinking and understand the ways in which six different skills combine to enable effective thinking.
Three allow us to fully understand a problem; three more give us the tools to solve it. Together, these six skills make up the **PACIER** model of critical thinking. They are:

ANALYSIS – understanding how an argument is built
EVALUATION – exploring the strengths and weaknesses of an argument
INTERPRETATION – understanding issues of meaning

CREATIVE THINKING – coming up with new ideas and fresh connections
PROBLEM-SOLVING – producing strong solutions
REASONING – creating strong arguments

To find out more, visit **WWW.MACAT.COM.**

CRITICAL THINKING AND *THE SOCIAL CONTRACT*

Primary critical thinking skill: CREATIVE THINKING
Secondary critical thinking skill: REASONING

Few people can claim to have had minds as fertile and creative as the French philosopher Jean-Jacques Rousseau. One of the most influential political theorists of the modern age, he was also a composer and writer of opera, a novelist, and a memoirist whose *Confessions* ranks as one of the most striking works of autobiography ever written.

Like many creative thinkers, Rousseau was someone whose restless mind could not help questioning accepted orthodoxies and looking at matters from novel and innovative angles. His 1762 treatise *The Social Contract* does exactly that. Examining the nature and sources of legitimate political power, it crafted a closely reasoned and passionately persuasive argument for democracy at a time when the most widely accepted form of government was absolute monarchy, legitimised by religious beliefs about the divine right of kings and queens to rule. In France, the book was banned by worried Catholic censors; in Rousseau's native Geneva, it was both banned and burned. But history soon pushed Rousseau's ideas into the mainstream of political theory, with the French and American revolutions paving the way for democratic government to gain ground across the Western world.

Though it was precisely what got Rousseau's book banned at the time, the novel idea that all legitimate government rests on the will of the people is now recognised as the core principle of democratic freedom and represents, for many people, the highest of ideals.

ABOUT THE AUTHOR OF THE ORIGINAL WORK

Jean-Jacques Rousseau was born in Geneva in 1712. He first became famous as a composer, then as a writer and scholar, and was only later recognized as an important political thinker. He wrote about many different subjects, from music to education. His autobiography, *The Confessions*, was published after his death in 1778, and is famous for its startling honesty. Rousseau was well known during his lifetime, but his ideas were controversial, and his 1762 work *The Social Contract* was banned in France and Geneva when first published. Today, he is widely considered to be one of the most important minds in the history of Western political thought.

ABOUT THE AUTHOR OF THE ANALYSIS

James Hill did his postgraduate research in political economy at King's College London.

ABOUT MACAT

GREAT WORKS FOR CRITICAL THINKING

Macat is focused on making the ideas of the world's great thinkers accessible and comprehensible to everybody, everywhere, in ways that promote the development of enhanced critical thinking skills.

It works with leading academics from the world's top universities to produce new analyses that focus on the ideas and the impact of the most influential works ever written across a wide variety of academic disciplines. Each of the works that sit at the heart of its growing library is an enduring example of great thinking. But by setting them in context – and looking at the influences that shaped their authors, as well as the responses they provoked – Macat encourages readers to look at these classics and game-changers with fresh eyes. Readers learn to think, engage and challenge their ideas, rather than simply accepting them.

'Macat offers an amazing first-of-its-kind tool for interdisciplinary learning and research. Its focus on works that transformed their disciplines and its rigorous approach, drawing on the world's leading experts and educational institutions, opens up a world-class education to anyone.'

Andreas Schleicher
Director for Education and Skills, Organisation for Economic
Co-operation and Development

'Macat is taking on some of the major challenges in university education … They have drawn together a strong team of active academics who are producing teaching materials that are novel in the breadth of their approach.'

Prof Lord Broers,
former Vice-Chancellor of the University of Cambridge

'The Macat vision is exceptionally exciting. It focuses upon new modes of learning which analyse and explain seminal texts which have profoundly influenced world thinking and so social and economic development. It promotes the kind of critical thinking which is essential for any society and economy.
This is the learning of the future.'

Rt Hon Charles Clarke, former UK Secretary of State for Education

'The Macat analyses provide immediate access to the critical conversation surrounding the books that have shaped their respective discipline, which will make them an invaluable resource to all of those, students and teachers, working in the field.'

Professor William Tronzo, University of California at San Diego

WAYS IN TO THE TEXT

KEY POINTS

- Jean-Jacques Rousseau (1712–78) is considered one of the West's most important political thinkers.

- He argued that the only legitimate form of government was rule by the people.

- His 1762 work *The Social Contract* was important in offering radical ideas for the time.

Who Is Jean-Jacques Rousseau?

Jean-Jacques Rousseau, the author of *The Social Contract* (1762), was born in the Swiss city of Geneva in 1712. He lived a varied and illustrious life, first gaining fame as a composer and then as a writer and scholar, one of the most important political thinkers in Europe. Rousseau wrote about many different subjects, from music to education. In 1752, he composed a very popular opera, *The Village Soothsayer*, and in 1761 published his novel *Julie, or the New Heloise*, one of the eighteenth century's most admired works of literature. After his death in 1778, Rousseau's autobiography *The Confessions* was published in 1782; it is famous for its open and frank account of his life.

Rousseau is widely held to be one of the most important thinkers in Western political thought. His ideas about what makes a political system legitimate and his commitment to democracy*—a system of government in which power resides in the hands of the people, usually exercised through the election of representatives—were revolutionary and controversial at the time. In particular, Rousseau's ideas concerning freedom of religion upset the Roman Catholic* authorities in France, leading to *The Social Contract* being banned. Rousseau's ideas fared little better in his native Geneva, where the text was banned and burned.

Since the French Revolution* of 1789–99, in which the French monarchy* was overthrown and a republic* proclaimed, an event with global social and political repercussions, Rousseau's ideas have been criticized on the basis that they could be used to justify totalitarianism* and authoritarian* rule (forms of government that involve significant control of individuals by the state). Particularly controversial is Rousseau's idea of the general will* (rule by the people in the interest of the community as a whole), which critics argue could potentially be used to deny individuals their liberty.

What Does *The Social Contract* Say?

Rousseau's conclusion is that the only legitimate form of government is rule by the people. Rule by the people, or democracy, rests on the idea that only the people as a collective are sovereign*—the ultimate source of political authority. At the time this was a controversial position, particularly in France, Rousseau's home, then a place where power was held in the hands of the monarchy. For Rousseau, rule by the people is the only legitimate form of government, as it is the only one that allows individuals to be governed while remaining free—a property of the exercise of the general will.

Rousseau suggests that the people, as a collective body, will make decisions in line with the general will. To act in accordance with the general will is to make decisions in the interest of the whole of society. Instead of acting as individuals pursuing their own interests, people will come together under the general will, thinking of themselves as a whole and acting in the interests of that whole. Rousseau goes on to argue that any individual who does not act in line with the general will would be forced to do so. Despite this he continues to argue that even if people are forced to behave in accordance with the general will this will not reduce their freedom; to act in accordance with the general will is to consent to be limited by the terms of what Rousseau calls *the social contract.**

The social contract is an agreement that individuals enter into allowing them to leave the state of nature*—a concept describing the situation before society and the state came into existence, usually presumed to be dangerous and chaotic—and enter into a civil society bound by laws. In doing so, individuals give up perfect freedom to gain peace and security.

In *The Social Contract* Rousseau sets out the conditions under which he believes individuals would be willing to move from the state of nature into a political system, that is to submit themselves to being coerced by others through the social contract. Rousseau suggests that a key feature of an acceptable social contract is democratic rule, favoring a form of democracy known as direct democracy* where the people themselves meet to debate and pass the laws that will govern them.

Rousseau's view is that humankind is naturally good and that it is the system of government that corrupts us; bad political systems produce wickedness in individuals. This is why he is so keen to establish a political system that does not corrupt the individual. His argument has been incredibly important for Western political thought and he is widely considered to be one of the most influential political thinkers of the last 250 years. He provides intriguing and sometimes difficult answers to the most fundamental questions we can ask about government and society.

Why Does *The Social Contract* Matter?

While *The Social Contract* might not provide all the answers for any student intrigued by the questions that Rousseau asks, it is as an important starting point for thinking about important concepts such as coercion* (the use of force to make an individual act in a particular way), freedom, and government. Almost every important political thinker since Rousseau has either been inspired by, or reacted against, the arguments proposed by *The Social Contract*. Rousseau has influenced almost every major school of political thought over the last two and a half centuries.

The Social Contract was written during a period of intense change in political thought. The Enlightenment*—a movement in European history in the seventeenth and eighteenth centuries, when ideas about individual freedom and scientific investigation began to dominate society—involved a new interest in applying reason (logical, objective thought) to matters of science, as well as politics and morality. People began to question the Church's authority in matters of morality, and to question the authority of monarchs (kings and queens) whose rule was supported by the Church. These circumstances prompted Rousseau to ask questions that related to the deepest foundation of any political system: What is it that individuals owe each other when they come together to form a society? And why should people in societies obey those that rule over them? The text remains relevant because these are questions that curious people still think about. In *The Social Contract*, Rousseau provides his answers to the problems of society and authority, but there is plenty of room for readers to come to their own conclusions.

While Rousseau's idea that the only legitimate form of government is rule by the people no longer seems like an unusual claim, at the time of publication he was challenging many established ideas concerning power and authority. These include the argument put forward by the English political theorist Thomas Hobbes* that individuals must completely submit themselves to a ruler in order to live in peace, or the ancient Greek philosopher Aristotle's* claim that humankind is naturally unequal as some people are born to rule and others to be ruled.

Rousseau's new ideas about democracy have influenced a great number of political and cultural movements ranging from the French Revolution and the literary and artistic current of Romanticism* to the socialist* movements of the twentieth century, calling for trade and industry to be conducted in order to ensure social equality.

SECTION 1
INFLUENCES

MODULE 1
THE AUTHOR AND THE HISTORICAL CONTEXT

KEY POINTS

- *The Social Contract* (1762) remains one of the most significant pieces of political philosophy ever produced, addressing the fundamental issue of what makes a government legitimate.

- Rousseau's experiences of living under different types of government across Europe were a large influence on the ideas in *The Social Contract*.

- Changes to forms of government across Europe, in particular the ending of absolute monarchy* (the rule of kings and queens), had a significant impact on the text.

Why Read This Text?

Jean-Jacques Rousseau's *The Social Contract* (1762) is "one of the most important and influential pieces of political philosophy ever written."[1] It addresses fundamental questions: When is coercion* (forcible persuasion) of individuals legitimate, and under what circumstances should individuals obey their rulers?[2] These questions were not only relevant when Rousseau published the text in 1762; they will be relevant as long as individuals are required to be bound by a system of laws.

Rousseau uses an approach different from much Western liberal* political thought (that is, political thought emphasizing the importance of liberty), which has tended to think only in terms of the state oppressing individuals, and not other citizens being responsible for oppression. As the political and social philosophy scholar Christopher

> **❝** I have entered on an enterprise which is without precedent, and will have no imitator. **❞**
>
> Jean-Jacques Rousseau, *The Confessions*

Bertram* argues, "Rousseau's focus on the common or public interest, and the need to intervene to protect it against private sectional interests, marks a very different emphasis in his work from the one we often find in the Anglo-American liberal tradition."[3] For Rousseau, challenges to a society's freedom could come from people included in that society and rulers alike.

Instead of just thinking about the relationship between the individual and the state, Rousseau argues that individual freedom could be limited by private power—the power of other individuals as well as the power of the state.[4] As such, "Rousseau's importance lies in his trying to think through what is needed if individuals are to escape becoming subject to the private wills of other individuals."[5]

Author's Life

Rousseau had a colorful and varied life. He was born in 1712 in the Swiss city of Geneva and was brought up by his father after his mother died in childbirth. Rousseau's father, a watchmaker, inspired Rousseau's twin passions: literature and nature.[6] When he was 15, Rousseau went for a walk outside Geneva but when he returned the city gates were shut and he decided to leave the city.[7] Over the next 10 years he became the pupil and lover of Madame de Warens,* a teacher and Roman Catholic* convert.

In 1742, Rousseau moved to Paris to promote his work, in particular a new method of musical notation and his comic play *Narcissus*.[8] He met the French writer Denis Diderot* and was commissioned by him to write articles on music and political economy for Diderot's *Encyclopédie*￼* (his general encyclopedia). This was an important meeting for Rousseau as it gave him the opportunity to write on subjects other than music, starting him on a path that would culminate in *The Social Contract*.

Rousseau wrote on a range of subjects, from arts and sciences, through literary works, to discussions of education. Rousseau's autobiography *The Confessions*, written in 1769, was published in 1782, four years after his death.

The Social Contract was influenced by Rousseau's experience of living under different political systems: the monarchy* in France,[9] the Republic of Venice* (a historical state in north-eastern Italy, where he worked for the French ambassador), and the city-state of Geneva.[10] His life in Geneva most greatly influenced *The Social Contract*; on the title page he declares himself to be "A Citizen of Geneva,"[11] and his experience of the political system operating there inspired his argument about what a legitimate political system should be.

Author's Background

Rousseau "lived through a period of profound social and political change."[12] He was born less than three years before the end of the powerful monarchy of the French king Louis XIV* and died only a decade before the French Revolution* of 1789–99,[13] a period of great political change that resulted in the overthrow of the monarchy altogether. The novel was a new form of literature at the time;[14] this also helped to expose people to new ideas and concepts in a way that had never happened previously. These new ideas were also discussed by philosophers such as Scotland's David Hume* and Germany's notably influential Immanuel Kant,* who "were making seminal contributions to questions of metaphysics,* religion, economics, morality and political theory"[15] around the same time as Rousseau ("metaphysics" here refers to the branch of philosophy dealing with fundamental questions of existence).

The Social Contract was molded by the changing political and social culture of the time. Referencing feudalism,* a system in which status and political power are tied up with land ownership, the Rousseau scholar Christopher D.Wraight* argues that this changing culture was a product of a more peaceful period of history: "Freed from the destructive religious conflict and lingering feudalism of the [seventeenth] century, educated men (and it was mostly men) in a comparatively wealthy and peaceful age were able to bend their efforts towards the creation and refinement of new inventions in a whole range of disciplines."[16]

New ideas about reason and rational thought were then used to "question long-established political and religious conventions."[17] Many of Europe's rulers used religious institutions to justify their authority, so questioning the Church also meant questioning the legitimacy of the governments of the time. *The Social Contract*'s arguments can best be understood within this context of dissent.

These events certainly influenced Rousseau's work, and his work also played a significant part in changing the way people thought. In *Julie, or the New Heloise* he put forward new ideas about morality; in *The Social Contract* he attempted to lay down the conditions for a legitimate political society. His work was motivated by the political changes he experienced, and he used this motivation to contribute to the debates around him. As Wraight comments, "Rather than simply reflecting the tastes and preoccupations of his age, he helped to challenge and shape them."[18]

Rousseau wanted to change existing views about what a legitimate government entailed, and in some ways he succeeded. After the publication of *The Social Contract* in 1762, Rousseau's ideas about political systems became so popular that he was asked to draft a constitution for Corsica and to offer advice on a new political system for Poland. Both countries also asked him to act as their legislator (a position associated with the making of laws).[19]

NOTES

1 Christopher D. Wraight, *Rousseau's 'The Social Contract': A Reader's Guide* (New York: Continuum, 2008), vii.

2 Matthew Simpson, *Rousseau: A Guide for the Perplexed* (New York: Continuum, 2007), 81.

3 Christopher Bertram, *Routledge Philosophy GuideBook to Rousseau and the Social Contract* (London: Routledge, 2004), 203.

4 Bertram, *Routledge Philosophy GuideBook*, 203.

5 Bertram, *Routledge Philosophy GuideBook*, 203.

6 Robert Wolker, *Rousseau: A Very Short Introduction* (Oxford: Oxford University Press, 2001), 2.

7 Simpson, *Rousseau*, 5.

8 Wolker, *Rousseau*, 6.

9 During his time in France, Rousseau lived under the rule of Louis XV, an absolute monarch.*

10 Simpson, *Rousseau*, 12.

11 Wraight, Rousseau's *'The Social Contract'*, 20.

12 Wraight, *Rousseau's 'The Social Contract'*, 1.

13 Wraight, *Rousseau's 'The Social Contract'*, 1.

14 Wraight, *Rousseau's 'The Social Contract'*, 1.

15 Wraight, *Rousseau's 'The Social Contract'*, 1.

16 Wraight, *Rousseau's 'The Social Contract'*, 2.

17 Wraight, *Rousseau's 'The Social Contract'*, 2.

18 Wraight, *Rousseau's 'The Social Contract'*, 1.

19 Wolker, *Rousseau*, 18.

MODULE 2
ACADEMIC CONTEXT

KEY POINTS

- The major concern within political thought when *The Social Contract* was first published was the nature of legitimate government: what gives a government the right to rule over people.

- Some thinkers argued that authoritarian* governments (governments that exert a significant amount of control over individuals) could be legitimate, either for practical reasons or due to natural inequalities among people.

- In *The Social Contract*, Rousseau sought to address these points and make his own argument about the nature of a fair and just government.

The Work in its Context

The most important intellectual tendency in Jean-Jacques Rousseau's time was the Enlightenment,* an intellectual current emphasizing the importance of reason;[1] its influence is detectable in his *The Social Contract*.

Reason requires that knowledge be produced through the logical and methodical testing of concepts. In this light, the Enlightenment was associated with great advances in the field of science, leading to new inventions that facilitated the Industrial Revolution*—the large-scale movement from agricultural to industrial economies, and the beginning of modern capitalist* society in Europe and America. Capitalism is a system in which trade and industry are conducted for the sake of private profit.

Ideas about human rationality were also used to question the political and religious beliefs of the time.[2] There was a great deal of

❝ No other figure of the Enlightenment was more hostile to the course that political civilization had taken and at the same time so proud of his political identity. ❞

Robert Wolker, *Rousseau: A Very Short Introduction*

criticism of the Church's dominant position in society, and much of this criticism aimed directly at eroding the Church's power.[3]

In *The Social Contract*, Rousseau attempts to answer questions concerning what form of government was legitimate and when individuals should obey their rulers. The work reflects the Enlightenment spirit and faith in human reason. Rousseau rejects the idea that monarchs* had a divine right* to rule, and does not accept that some people were naturally superior to others.[4] For him, "the only just sovereign* to rule over a society is the collective will of the citizens themselves."[5] A society's leaders should reflect the desires and needs of the people who make up that society.

Although this is in keeping with Enlightenment ideas, other parts of Rousseau's work appear to reject Enlightenment thinking. "In the *Discourse on the Sciences and Arts*, Rousseau draws a parallel between intellectual progress and the decline of virtue."[6] In other words, Rousseau can be viewed as "a supporter of the Enlightenment project as well as a critic."[7]

Overview of the Field

The four thinkers that dominated thought about the nature of government at the time were the political philosophers Thomas Hobbes* and John Locke* of England, Hugo Grotius* of the Netherlands, and the ancient Greek philosopher Aristotle.*

Hobbes, Grotius, and Aristotle argued that authoritarian rule was a legitimate form of government. In his book *Leviathan* (1651), Hobbes argued that societies needed strong governments because they would otherwise become a bloody war of "all against all" in what he calls "the state of nature."* For Hobbes, strong government is essential to bring order. Individuals act in their self-interest by giving up their freedom to be ruled by a sovereign with complete authority over society, because they are then less at risk from other individuals.

In *On the Law of War and Peace* (1625), Grotius argued that rulers had rights over their subjects, and that this meant even oppressive regimes could be considered legitimate.[8] In his *Politics* (350 B.C.E.), Aristotle argued that "certain classes in society are more inherently suited to rule than others."[9] According to Aristotle, some people cannot use their freedom in an effective way and need to be ruled by others with superior abilities.[10] Rousseau's aim was to demonstrate why these arguments were incorrect, and in doing so to establish the foundations for "fair and just governments."[11]

Locke, however, proposed an argument in favor of government that did not justify authoritarian rule. His argument is that the only legitimate justification for the authority of any ruler is that they protect the rights of the individuals that make up society.[12] In the state of nature, individuals are aware that there is the potential for arguments and disagreements, and in order to avoid this they agree to submit to a ruler who is able to settle disputes. The authority of the ruler comes from the consent of the governed. Following the creation of this society, writes Locke, "men gain three things which they lacked in the State of Nature: laws, judges to adjudicate laws, and the executive power necessary to enforce these laws."[13] If a ruler does not protect the rights of the individual in society, they have the right to rebel and return to the state of nature.

Academic Influences

Rousseau's political thought is certainly influenced by the Enlightenment.[14] As much as *The Social Contract* is not meant to be an account of the ideal society, it contains a practical element.[15] This approach is similar to that taken by political thinkers such as the Florentine political theorist Niccolò Machiavelli.* In his *The Prince*, Machiavelli sought to give practical advice to rulers, in the same way Rousseau attempts to provide a realistic and attainable outline for a just political system in *The Social Contract*.

Rousseau was also part of the tradition of social contract* theory. This theory is based on the idea that political obligations are decided by agreement between individuals within a particular society. This agreement usually involves individuals giving up some of their liberty in order to live in a peaceful society. Rousseau's ideas about society were influenced by the social contract theory of thinkers such as Hobbes and Locke. From Hobbes, Rousseau took the idea that the basis of society could be voluntary agreement—the principle that individuals agree to be ruled in order to secure the advantages of living in a society under the rule of law. Locke argued that the fundamental purpose of a society was to protect the rights of its citizens, and that this could be achieved through the social contract setting out the relationship between the sovereign and the people. Although Rousseau agreed with this idea in general, he argues that the contract should be between everyone in society, rather than between a ruler and the rest of society alone: for him, the people themselves are sovereign.[16]

NOTES

1 James Delaney, *Starting with Rousseau* (New York: Continuum, 2009), 1.

2 Christopher D. Wraight, *Rousseau's 'The Social Contract': A Reader's Guide* (New York: Continuum, 2008), 2.

3 Wraight, *Rousseau's 'The Social Contract'*, 2

4 Delaney, *Starting with Rousseau*, 2.

5 Delaney, *Starting with Rousseau*, 2.

6 Delaney, *Starting with Rousseau*, 2.

7   Delaney, *Starting with Rousseau*, 3.

8   Wraight, *Rousseau's 'The Social Contract'*, 25.

9   Wraight, *Rousseau's 'The Social Contract'*, 26.

10   Wraight, *Rousseau's 'The Social Contract'*, 26.

11   Wraight, *Rousseau's 'The Social Contract'*, 21.

12   Celeste Friend, "Social Contract Theory," *Internet Encyclopaedia of Philosophy*, 2004, http://www.iep.utm.edu/soc-cont/, accessed January 3, 2016.

13   Friend, *Social Contract Theory*.

14   Delaney, *Starting with Rousseau*, 2.

15   Christopher Bertram, *Routledge Philosophy GuideBook to Rousseau and the Social Contract* (London: Routledge, 2004), 41.

16   Daryl Worthington, "Rousseau's *The Social Contract*," *NewHistorian*, November 7, 2014, http://www.newhistorian.com/rousseaus-social-contract/1972/, accessed January 3, 2016.

MODULE 3
THE PROBLEM

KEY POINTS

- The main concern among scholars at the time of the publication of *The Social Contract* was the question of whether or not coercion* was justifiable, and in what circumstances.

- The main positions at the time justified coercion on the basis that without it there would be little chance of people living peacefully together.

- Rousseau rejects these arguments, proposing his own theory of justifiable coercion.

Core Question

The core question that Jean-Jacques Rousseau seeks to answer in *The Social Contract* is: If all types of government involve some degree of coercion, which forms of coercion are justifiable?[1] That is: What is required for the coercion of individuals to be considered legitimate, and under what circumstances are individuals morally obligated to obey their rulers?[2]

The issue was important because it related directly to debates of the time questioning absolute monarchy* (a type of government in which the monarch wields total power) and the Church. Rousseau sought to use reason to establish when coercion was legitimate, and, like the French writer Voltaire,* he questioned the divine right* of royalty to rule. This raised the question of what legitimate government *should* look like.

In his *Republic,* the ancient Greek philosopher Plato* had already addressed the issue of what makes the government of a society just. Rousseau was attempting to answer a question that was particularly

> ❝ Tranquility is found also in dungeons; but is that
> enough to make them desirable places to live in? ❞
>
> Jean-Jacques Rousseau, *The Social Contract*

relevant at the time, but was also one of the enduring issues within political philosophy.

The Participants

The English political philosopher Thomas Hobbes* suggested in his book *Leviathan* that in the state of nature*—a hypothetical world before laws and governments—people would live under "continual fear, and danger of violent death; and the life of man, solitary, poor, nasty, brutish, and short."[3] Hobbes's argument, in the tradition of social contract* theory (the theory that societies are regulated by contractual agreements between people), was that "it is in the populace's interest to sign over a large portion of their freedom to a powerful sovereign."*[4] This allows the powerful sovereign to ensure that society is peaceful and stable, achieved through the use of authoritarian* powers that enable the sovereign to make laws and control the military.[5] Hobbes argued that people "may not legally challenge their form of government, even if they find it oppressive and cruel."[6]

In his *On the Law of War and Peace*, the Dutch jurist Hugo Grotius* argued that a just society could be based on a covenant:* "an agreement between all members of the society to live under rules they agree on."[7] As such, Grotius argues, "a people may give itself up to a king."[8] He thought that an individual could under certain circumstances agree to enslave themselves, and that, similarly, "a whole people could consent to obey a king in the same manner."[9] This covenant was most likely to occur at times of war or invasion and sovereign authority is justified on the grounds that "there is a contract between conquerors and those they defeat, whereby the vanquished agree to accept authority in return for their lives."[10] This account of a people voluntarily submitting to a monarch is not dissimilar to Hobbes's argument.

In his *Two Treatises of Government*, the English political philosopher John Locke* proposed an argument that did not justify authoritarian rule but was instead in favor of a government that protected the rights of citizens. The government could claim legitimacy through the popular consent of those that it ruled over: this is Locke's concept of popular sovereignty.* Locke believed that in the state of nature it was possible for disputes to arise (especially about property), even though each individual still had an obligation to behave morally, even in the absence of government. Locke used the same contractual method as Hobbes to argue that by establishing some kind of civil authority, the government would be able to prevent these disputes escalating into a state of war so that all would be better off. For Locke, society is formed when people come together and give up their power to punish those who transgress against them, instead giving that power to a government. The key aspect to this process is that individuals consent to be governed. Because the fundamental aim of the social contract is to protect the rights of people, if the government stops protecting the rights of the people, the people are justified in rebelling against it. This may involve a return to the state of nature, which Locke suggests could be preferable to an oppressive government.[11]

The Contemporary Debate

Rousseau did not have a personal relationship with the other thinkers who had addressed this question: they made their contribution to the debate over a century before Rousseau wrote *The Social Contract*, and in the case of Aristotle 2000 years earlier. Hobbes published *Leviathan* in 1651, Grotius's work *On the Law of War and Peace* dated back to 1625, and Locke's *Two Treatises* was published in 1689.

Rousseau does, however, directly address the arguments associated with Hobbes and Grotius respectively. While he does not directly mention Locke, his engagement with his theories is implicit in his argument. The beginning of *The Social Contract* involves Rousseau attempting to refute these arguments, as he believed them to be false theories of what makes a government just. His aim was to dismiss these competing theories in order to clear the ground so that he could propose his own argument for what makes a legitimate government.

Although Rousseau disagreed with the arguments put forward by these thinkers, their ideas were still very important for the development of his own thought. All three proposed original and thought-provoking arguments that aided Rousseau's own system of thought. Rousseau was deeply influenced by the contractual approach used by Hobbes in *Leviathan* as a means of justifying coercion, for example.

NOTES

1   Matthew Simpson, *Rousseau: A Guide for the Perplexed* (New York: Continuum, 2007), 81.

2   Simpson, *Rousseau*, 81.

3   Thomas Hobbes, *Leviathan* (Oxford: Oxford University Press, 1996), 87.

4   Christopher D. Wraight, *Rousseau's 'The Social Contract': A Reader's Guide* (New York: Continuum, 2008), 32.

5   Wraight, *Rousseau's 'The Social Contract'*, 32.

6   Wraight, *Rousseau's 'The Social Contract'*, 32.

7   Wraight, *Rousseau's 'The Social Contract'*, 29.

8   Michel Rosenfeld, *Constitutionalism, Identity, Difference, and Legitimacy: Theoretical Perspectives* (Durham, NC: Duke University Press, 1994), 161.

9   Robert Wolker, *Rousseau: A Very Short Introduction* (Oxford: Oxford University Press, 2001), 75.

10 Christopher Bertram, *Routledge Philosophy GuideBook to Rousseau and the* Social Contract (London: Routledge, 2004), 67.

11 Celeste Friend, "Social Contract Theory," *Internet Encyclopaedia of Philosophy*, 2004, http://www.iep.utm.edu/soc-cont/, accessed January 3, 2016.

MODULE 4
THE AUTHOR'S CONTRIBUTION

KEY POINTS

- Rousseau argued that a legitimate political system could only exist if the people were sovereign*—that is, in control of their fate.

- This was a rejection of previous arguments claiming that in some circumstances it was morally acceptable for people to be oppressed by a ruler.

- While Rousseau's argument was original, it drew on the ideas of thinkers such as the ancient Greek philosopher Aristotle* and the English philosophers Thomas Hobbes* and John Locke.*

Author's Aims

The broad question Jean-Jacques Rousseau attempts to answer in *The Social Contract* is: When is political authority legitimate? He begins with the line "My purpose is to consider if, in political society, there can be any legitimate and sure principle of government, taking men as they are and laws as they might be."[1] He approaches this question in a particular way; "Rousseau's aim in *The Social Contract* is to reconcile freedom and authority so that each person both enjoys the protection of the state but obeys 'only himself and remains as free as before.'"[2]

Rousseau took this approach believing that in the state of nature*—a hypothetical world before laws and governments— "people are by nature benign creatures … However, poorly formed society tends to corrupt these impulses."[3] This is the background to the famous opening line of the first chapter: "Man was born free, and he is everywhere in chains."[4]

> ❝ In one direction at least Rousseau's influence was a steady one: he discredited force as a basis for the State, convinced men that authority was legitimate only when founded in rational consent and that no arguments from passing expediency could justify a government in disregarding individual freedom or in failing to promote social equality. ❞
>
> Kingsley Martin, *French Liberal Thought in the Eighteenth Century*

Rousseau believes that illegitimate forms of government have corrupted and trapped people. His project, though, is not to explain how these chains can be removed; instead his aim is to set out "what kind of chains, if any, can be morally justified."[5] Rousseau sums up his aim by saying, "How did this transformation come about? I do not know. How can it be made legitimate? That question I believe I can answer."[6]

The argument of *The Social Contract* is organized into four separate books. The first deals with the foundations of a just society and rejects previous justifications by other theorists. The second sets out what kind of legal system it would use. The third looks at the powers that the government should have, and the final book concerns other issues of social organization such as the role of religion.[7]

Approach

The approach Rousseau takes is within the social contract* tradition as used by thinkers such as Hobbes and Locke—the idea that society is regulated by contractual agreements between people, so that perfect freedom is given up in exchange for peace and security under governance. However, Rousseau takes an approach that was as unique as it was controversial, as he starts from the premise that all people are born free and equal, writing that "no person has natural authority over another and that all people are 'created equal.'"[8] At the time, this ran contrary to the common belief that "God [granted] to some people the authority to tell other people what to do."[9]

From this position of equality, Rousseau argues that legitimate government can only come from agreement: "But the social order is a sacred right which serves as the basis of all other rights. And it is not a natural right, it must be one founded on covenants."*[10] Rousseau explains that it is his aim in *The Social Contract* to set out the circumstances in which individuals will allow themselves to be ruled and coerced by others.[11] This approach was in direct opposition to mainstream views at the time, rejecting, for example, the Greek philosopher Aristotle's idea that individuals are naturally unequal and some people are born to rule. Rousseau's view that people are fundamentally equal is also in opposition to the Dutch political philosopher Hugo Grotius's* view that a group of people can voluntarily give themselves up to a king in the same way that he believes a slave can voluntarily give themselves up to a master: such an agreement is not one made by equals, as "for that to be the case, both parties must come together in some sense as individuals of a comparable moral level."[12]

Contribution in Context

Rousseau's approach is highly original, and did not originate in any particular school of thought. Nevertheless, he was influenced by certain thinkers, even those he criticized. For example, at the start of *The Social Contract* Rousseau argues that the ties that bind together the individuals within a family should not be used as a model for individuals in a society.[13] Rousseau acknowledges "his profound debt to Aristotle on this subject and largely rephrases what Aristotle had already said."[14] He also takes on Locke's argument "that legitimate government among persons morally equal to one another was established by consent rather than acquired naturally."[15] However, many of Rousseau's ideas came about in reaction against the arguments of the time, particularly those of Hobbes and Grotius.

Elements of *The Social Contract* relate to Rousseau's earlier works of political theory. An issue of key significance is Rousseau's belief that humans in the state of nature are benign beings, but bad and illegitimate forms of government corrupt people.[16] This claim has its roots in his earlier work *Discourse on Inequality* (1755), in which he developed his argument that "a healthy desire for the preservation of our self is the basis for all our other drives."[17] The desire to preserve our self outside of the state of nature can result in this harmless instinct being corrupted.[18]

NOTES

1   Jean-Jacques Rousseau, *The Social Contract* (London: Penguin Classics, 1968), 49.

2   Gerald F. Gaus and Fred D'Agostino, *The Routledge Companion to Social and Political Philosophy* (New York: Routledge: 2013), 90.

3   Christopher D. Wraight, *Rousseau's 'The Social Contract': A Reader's Guide* (New York: Continuum, 2008), 21.

4   Rousseau, *The Social Contract*, 49.

5   Matthew Simpson, *Rousseau: A Guide for the Perplexed* (New York: Continuum, 2007), 81.

6   Rousseau, *The Social Contract*, 49.

7   Wraight, *Rousseau's 'The Social Contract'*, 20.

8   Simpson, *Rousseau*, 81.

9   Simpson, *Rousseau*, 81–2.

10 Rousseau, *The Social Contract*, 50.

11 Rousseau, *The Social Contract*, 50.

12 Wraight, *Rousseau's 'The Social Contract'*, 20.

13 Rousseau, *The Social Contract*, 51.

14 Robert Wolker, *Rousseau: A Very Short Introduction* (Oxford: Oxford University Press, 2001), 74.

15 Wolker, *Rousseau*, 74.

16 Wraight, *Rousseau's 'The Social Contract'*, 12.

17 Wraight, *Rousseau's 'The Social Contract'*, 15.

18 Wraight, *Rousseau's 'The Social Contract'*, 15.

SECTION 2
IDEAS

MODULE 5
MAIN IDEAS

KEY POINTS

- Rousseau's key themes are his concept of the general will* (the needs and desires of the people as a whole) and his argument for democratic* popular sovereignty* (a state under which people, not their rulers, are the source of political power).

- He argues that the only legitimate government is a democratic government guided by the general will.

- The main ideas are presented in Book One of *The Social Contract*; he spends the rest of the book justifying these arguments.

Key Themes

Jean-Jacques Rousseau argues in *The Social Contract* that a government can only be legitimate (that is, acceptable and justified) if it comes about through the consent of the governed. Rousseau seeks to answer the "question of what political arrangements people would consent to under free and fair conditions."[1] In other words, what should the terms of the social contract*—the set of agreements between people made to regulate society—be to ensure a legitimate government?

Like the political philosopher Thomas Hobbes,* Rousseau believes that people have to form a society under the rule of law in order to guarantee their personal safety. But he faces a challenge: How can people submit themselves to being bound by laws and still be free? Rousseau's solution is the concept of the general will, concerning the "motivation to do what is in the interests of the community as a whole."[2] By following the general will, Rousseau argues that the

> **❝** It was Rousseau who developed the concept of sovereignty of the people, and he was the first to insist upon the fitness and right of the ordinary people to participate in the political system as full citizens. **❞**
>
> Ian Adams and R. W. Dyson, *Fifty Major Political Thinkers*

sovereign* (the source of authority and law)[3] will be able to rule in a just manner. Individuals remain free under this arrangement because "instead of regarding ourselves as individuals, we regard ourselves first and foremost as parts of a whole."[4] Freedom is an attribute of communities, not of individual people.

Rousseau then discusses the idea of sovereignty, putting forward the case that the people must be sovereign, meaning that legitimate rule has to be democratic, being based on debate and discussion between all members of society. As one commentator writes, "This was obviously a controversial argument at the time, especially in France, with its tradition of grand monarchy."*[5] Organizing society democratically will enable people to exercise the general will. Rousseau suggests that anyone who goes against the general will must "be 'forced to be free.' In practical terms, this means they will be compelled to act in accordance with the decision of the entire community."[6] Rousseau sets out these positions in Book One of *The Social Contract*; the rest of the work justifies and explains this initial argument.

Exploring the Ideas

Rousseau's notion of the general will is one of his most difficult and important ideas. The British scholar Christopher D. Wraight* comments, "The idea of the 'general will' is one of the most perplexing ideas in the entire *Social Contract*, even though it is essential to the coherence of the whole."[7] The general will can best be understood as the "public interest or common good that the sovereign of every state ought to promote."[8] One of Rousseau's main aims is to explain how an individual can be free while being governed. The general will plays a crucial role in explaining how this is possible. As Rousseau suggests, "Each of us puts into the community his person and all his powers under the supreme direction of the general will; and in a body we receive each member as an indivisible part of the whole."[9] By the community acting as a whole, under the general will, no individual's liberty is undermined.

As pointed out previously, however, Rousseau also claimed that, if anyone acted against the general will, they would be made to go along with the community's decision. This appears to contradict Rousseau's aim of establishing "a form of political association which provides security while still preserving as much freedom as an individual has in the state of nature."*[10] The solution to this puzzle comes in the second book of *The Social Contract*, where Rousseau makes a distinction between "natural liberty" and "civil liberty." The former is the liberty people have in the state of nature—in an ungoverned situation; the latter is the liberty people have in a political system. Rousseau argues that this second form of liberty is always in accordance with the general will.[11]

The people themselves should pursue the general will as "sovereign" (that is, as masters of their own fate). For Rousseau, this did not just mean that representatives should vote on laws; the people themselves should debate and decide.[12] In other words, he favors direct democracy* (where the electorate are directly involved in the decision-making process) rather than representative democracy* (where the people are represented by professional politicians): "Any law which the people has not ratified in person is null; it is not law at all."[13] However; Rousseau's conception of sovereignty does allow for an executive* (law-enforcing) branch of government run by elected representatives. Only the process of making law requires direct involvement from citizens. Rousseau refers to this executive branch as "The Prince" and it rules in tandem with the Sovereign (the people); as he argues, "they are the necessary elements of any well-ordered society and … they define the character of political life within the social pact."[14]

Language and Expression

Throughout *The Social Contract*, Rousseau uses difficult and technical language. While the term "the general will" is never defined precisely, it has been suggested that Rousseau's failure to provide a precise definition was deliberate. The political science professor David Lay Williams* observes, "One possible reason he never develops a systemic account of the general will is simply that the term was already well known to most of the book's target audience of erudite [learned] political thinkers."[15] Others, however, have argued that Rousseau deliberately uses vague language when discussing concepts such as the general will as a way of avoiding close scrutiny of his ideas.[16]

Because of Rousseau's somewhat vague use of language, *The Social Contract* is a book simultaneously straightforward and difficult to understand. On one level, the vagueness allows readers to interpret the ideas Rousseau puts forward on their own terms; but the ambiguity also means that it can be very difficult to define exactly what Rousseau means in some circumstances. This does not appear to have had much of an impact on the reach or reception of *The Social Contract*, however, as it continues to be one of the most read and debated works of political philosophy.

Rousseau's use of language in *The Social Contract* was quite innovative, often adding to the academic vocabulary of the time: "Every reader of Rousseau needs to know that 'social' was an unfamiliar word when he used it in the title of the *Social Contract*."[17]

We must thank Rousseau for the term "social contract theory"; he was a thinker "in the forefront of a movement to isolate what he called … the "social system."[18]

NOTES

1   Matthew Simpson, *Rousseau: A Guide for the Perplexed* (New York: Continuum, 2007), 83.

2   Christopher D. Wraight, *Rousseau's 'The Social Contract': A Reader's Guide* (New York: Continuum, 2008), 40.

3   Simpson, *Rousseau*, 86.

4   James Delaney, *Starting with Rousseau* (New York: Continuum, 2009), 121.

5   Simpson, *Rousseau*, 87.

6   Wraight, *Rousseau's 'The Social Contract'*, 40.

7   Wraight, *Rousseau's 'The Social Contract'*, 40.

8   Robert Wolker, *Rousseau: A Very Short Introduction* (Oxford: Oxford University Press, 2001), 86.

9   Jean-Jacques Rousseau, *The Social Contract* (London: Penguin Classics, 1968), 61.

10 Wraight, *Rousseau's 'The Social Contract'*, 41.

11 Wraight, *Rousseau's 'The Social Contract'*, 43.

12 Simpson, *Rousseau*, 87.

13 Rousseau, *The Social Contract*, 141.

14 Simpson, *Rousseau*, 89.

15 David Lay Williams, *Rousseau's* Social Contract*: An Introduction* (Cambridge: Cambridge University Press: 2014), 245.

16 Wraight, *Rousseau's 'The Social Contract'*, 112.

17 Jean-Jacques Rousseau, *The Basic Political Writings*, trans. and ed. Donald A. Cress (Indianapolis, IN: Hackett Publishing, 2012), xxxii.

18 Rousseau, *The Basic Political Writings*, xxxii.

MODULE 6
SECONDARY IDEAS

KEY POINTS

- Rousseau argues that, under the social contract, individuals will be able to remain free; he also supports religious freedom as long as it does not threaten social stability.

- These secondary ideas are important as they support Rousseau's main argument concerning the sovereignty* of the people (their power to make their own decisions).

- The most important secondary idea is Rousseau's concept of freedom.

Other Ideas

One of the key features of Jean-Jacques Rousseau's project in *The Social Contract* is to explain how individuals can still be free under a government pursuing the general will.* To understand his argument, it is useful to consider his concept of freedom; for Rousseau, entering into the social contract* fundamentally changes people: "The passing from the state of nature* to the civil society produces a remarkable change in man; it puts justice as a rule of conduct in the place of instinct, and gives his actions the moral quality they previously lacked."[1] Rousseau suggests that, under these conditions, people start to use reason to make their decisions; as one commentator has put it. "'Moral freedom' was his term for this power of acting according to duty."[2]

One of the most significant debates during the Enlightenment* was related to the relationship between the Church and the state. Rousseau's discussion of religion and politics formed a crucial part of

> ❝ It is therefore essential, if the general will is to be able to express itself, that there should be no partial society within the State, and that each citizen should think only his own thoughts. ❞
>
> Jean-Jacques Rousseau, *The Social Contract*

his theory of what government under the social contract should look like. He suggested that people should have religious freedom as long as their views were not damaging to the community:[3] "Subjects have no duty to account to the sovereign for their beliefs except when those beliefs are important to the community."[4]

Exploring the Ideas

As the scholar Christopher D. Wraight* comments, "*The Social Contract* dictates that each member gives up their individual right to act as they choose in favor of the general will of the community."[5] In addition to this, the sovereign is allowed to act against anyone who behaves in a way that goes against the general will. "Rousseau," however, "argues that such a state of affairs is consistent with the freedom of every individual in the community being enhanced, rather than diminished."[6] The social contract makes people more free overall, rather than less. Rousseau argues that this is so because of the idea that "an individual is more ... free the more opportunities they have to enhance their life and pursue objectives which lead to beneficial outcomes."[7]

The freedom that comes with the social contract, however, is also a moral freedom since "the social pact ... enables people to act on the basis of their political duties rather than on the basis of drives that nature has ... forced upon them."[8] In other words, when people are forced to follow the general will, they are following the rules that they agreed to follow when they joined the social pact,[9] rather than blindly obeying their natural instincts. For Rousseau, then, there is a fundamental difference between feeling free and being free.[10] Freedom is not about being totally independent, but about the extent to which you are able to follow rational principles that you have previously agreed to: "The criterion for freedom is whether or not an action is in conformity with the law that one has erected over oneself."[11]

On the issue of the role of religion under the social contract, Rousseau suggests freedom of religion is allowable as long as it does not harm society. However, Rousseau goes on to suggest that in order to prevent people from acting selfishly, a society requires a "civil profession of faith with tenets stating that a providential God exists and that in the next life the good will be rewarded and the wicked punished."[12] He follows this up by suggesting, "Without being able to oblige anyone to believe these articles, the sovereign can banish from the state anyone who does not believe them."[13]

Although Rousseau valued freedom of religion, he thought that the most fundamental issue is to preserve society, meaning that "one cannot meaningfully have a right to something that tends towards the destruction of society."[14]

Overlooked

One element of *The Social Contract* that has been somewhat overlooked is the role of the lawgiver* (a person or organization that guides the people to follow the general will) in Rousseau's argument. This is not to say that critics have not engaged with the concept at all, but they have certainly given it less attention than other elements of Rousseau's thought, despite its potential significance. Being one of the more confusing aspects of Rousseau's system of thought, the concept of the lawgiver has generally been neglected.[15]

"Individuals must be obliged to subordinate their will to their reason; the public must be taught to recognize what it desires,"

Rousseau writes. "Hence the necessity of a lawgiver."[16] What he means by this is that in order for a society to succeed, the individuals within the society need to have some kind of common bond.[17] This cannot come from society itself but must come from outside. The source of this bond or spirit is the lawgiver.[18] Crucially, and somewhat confusingly, the lawgiver does not have a role in making the law; only the people as sovereign can do this.[19]

The lawgiver's role is to "guide the sovereign such that the pronouncements it passes are wise and efficacious."[20] The lawgiver cannot simply use reason to convince the people to act in this way, as it would be ineffective. Instead, the lawgiver must "resort to inspiring the people to assume the proper attitudes and social spirit via an indirect mechanism and, in some way, 'persuade without convincing.'"[21] The fact that this element of Rousseau's thought has been somewhat overlooked has not had a large effect on the significance of *The Social Contract*, because the other elements of his argument are so important within Western political thought.

NOTES

1   Jean-Jacques Rousseau, *The Social Contract* (London: Penguin Classics, 1968), 64.

2   Matthew Simpson, *Rousseau: A Guide for the Perplexed* (New York: Continuum, 2007), 90.

3   Simpson, *Rousseau*, 92.

4   Rousseau, *The Social Contract*, 185.

5   Christopher D. Wraight, *Rousseau's 'The Social Contract': A Reader's Guide* (New York: Continuum, 2008), 44.

6   Wraight, *Rousseau's 'The Social Contract'*, 44.

7   Wraight, *Rousseau's 'The Social Contract'*, 44.

8   Simpson, *Rousseau*, 91.

9   Simpson, *Rousseau*, 91.

10 Simpson, *Rousseau*, 91.

11 Simpson, *Rousseau*, 91.

12 Simpson, *Rousseau*, 92.

13 Rousseau, *The Social Contract*, 186.

14 Simpson, *Rousseau*, 92.

15 Wraight, *Rousseau's 'The Social Contract'*, 69.

16 Rousseau, *The Social Contract*, 83.

17 Simpson, *Rousseau*, 89.

18 Simpson, *Rousseau: A Guide for the Perplexed*, 89.

19 Simpson, *Rousseau: A Guide for the Perplexed*, 89.

20 Wraight, *Rousseau's 'The Social Contract'*, 77.

21 Wraight, *Rousseau's 'The Social Contract'*, 77.

MODULE 7
ACHIEVEMENT

KEY POINTS

- Rousseau gave a comprehensive account of the foundations of legitimate, morally acceptable government—though there are concerns about the extent to which his suggestions are practical.

- Rousseau was able to achieve this through thinking about the problems within the tradition of social contract* theory.

- Rousseau struggled with censorship: the book was banned in both France and Geneva.

Assessing the Argument

In *The Social Contract*, Jean-Jacques Rousseau was undoubtedly successful in putting forward his argument concerning the conditions required for legitimate government of the people. The philosophy scholar Christopher D. Wraight* comments, "What is beyond question is that, for good or ill, *The Social Contract* and other writings by Jean-Jacques Rousseau have profoundly influenced political theory and practice."[1] The largest issue facing Rousseau's account of a legitimate political system, however, is the issue of whether such a society is actually possible. The philosophy professor James Delaney* notes, "Rousseau's political philosophy, particularly as it relies on the notion of the general will,* and the state as one unified entity, leaves one with the question of practicality."[2]

The issue is that, even though Rousseau has managed to set out the conditions for legitimate government, it is not clear if this is truly achievable. His project was never meant to be utopian* (a perfect imaginary system); it was supposed to be a practical guide to creating

> 66 Together with Montesquieu,* Hume,* Smith,* and Kant* among his contemporaries, Rousseau has exerted the most profound influence on modern European intellectual history, perhaps even surpassing anyone else of his day. 99
>
> Robert Wolker, *Rousseau: A Very Short Introduction*

legitimate political institutions. If it is not possible to create a real political system in line with Rousseau's ideas, then he will not have achieved everything he set out to achieve.

Whether Rousseau's ideas are practical is a difficult puzzle to answer. For example, one criticism of his argument is that people "will *never* be able to abandon viewing ourselves first and foremost as individuals: not as parts of a whole."[3] However, his argument is based on the idea that people become selfish because they become corrupted by the political system they live in, and are not inherently individualistic. Under Rousseau's system, he believes, people would act in accordance with the general will—meaning that his conception of legitimate government would be achievable. The problem we face in assessing this claim is we can only find out by trying to put his ideas into action.

Achievement in Context

The Social Contract was an extremely controversial book when it was published. In France, controlled at the time by the monarchy* and the Roman Catholic* Church, the most controversial aspect of the book was Rousseau's argument about religion: "Any infringement on freedom of conscience," he writes, "is an illegitimate use of state power, except when absolutely required for public safety."[4] In other words, people should be free to decide their own beliefs, unless they are a threat to others.

This in itself was controversial, as it went against the wishes of powerful people at the time, who wanted to control religious beliefs and prioritize Roman Catholicism. Rousseau further upset the Catholic authorities in France with his claim that "one of the few legitimate constraints on the freedom of conscience is to outlaw Catholicism because the obedience that Catholics owe to the Pope is incompatible with the obedience they owe to their civil magistrates."[5] In other words, Rousseau argued that Catholics' loyalty to the pope— the head of this branch of the Christian religion—might conflict with their duty to be obedient to their government. This criticism led to the banning of *The Social Contract* in France. The work was also banned in Geneva, where the authorities ordered it to be burned.[6]

Possibly because of the strong reaction by the authorities, *The Social Contract* was not immediately a popular work. Although Rousseau himself became a very popular figure after his death in 1778, this was not because of his political thought.[7] Ten years before the French Revolution* of 1789–99, this began to change. As Wraight says, "Widespread famine, malnutrition and unemployment created an atmosphere of resentment among the bulk of the populace against the excess and luxury of monarchy."[8] Following the revolution, Rousseau's ideas became more popular: "His ideas of communal ownership and resistance to the tyranny of unelected monarchs were very much in tune with the views of the progressive factions in France fighting for change."[9]

Limitations

Rousseau attempts to address one of the most fundamental questions in political philosophy: How can individuals be free yet allow themselves to be constrained by a system of coercive* laws—that is, laws that they are forced to follow? It can be argued that this is a question not simply relevant to one time or place, but a question that will always have relevance as long as people live in organized societies.

It could also be argued that *The Social Contract* had more relevance at the time it was published than it does now, however. At the time of publication, many societies were ruled by absolute monarchs* (kings and queens with total power) and the people as a collective had little power. Rousseau's claim was that only when there is rule by the people could a society be considered legitimately governed—a powerful claim at the time, which contributed to controversy surrounding *The Social Contract* following its publication.

It should be noted that following the democratization* of many societies in modern times, this central claim has somewhat less relevance. In a similar manner, Rousseau's favoring of direct democracy* as the only legitimate form of government may only be true in certain contexts. In Europe, ideas such as individual liberty and autonomy* (personal freedom) are held in high regard, meaning that representative democracy* is seen as the right way to recognize these values. It also may be the case that Rousseau's argument may not be as relevant within cultures that hold different values.

NOTES

1   Christopher D. Wraight, *Rousseau's 'The Social Contract': A Reader's Guide* (New York: Continuum, 2008), 120.

2   James Delaney, *Starting with Rousseau* (New York: Continuum, 2009), 135.

3   Delaney, *Starting with Rousseau*, 135.

4   Matthew Simpson, *Rousseau: A Guide for the Perplexed* (New York: Continuum, 2007), 25.

5   Simpson, *Rousseau*, 25.

6   Simpson, *Rousseau*, 26.

7   Wraight, *Rousseau's 'The Social Contract'*, 121.

8   Wraight, *Rousseau's 'The Social Contract'*, 121.

9   Wraight, *Rousseau's 'The Social Contract'*, 122.

MODULE 8
PLACE IN THE AUTHOR'S WORK

KEY POINTS

- Given the extremely varied nature of Rousseau's academic output, it is difficult to suggest that there is an overall theme to his work.

- *The Social Contract* built on Rousseau's earlier works *Discourse on the Arts and Sciences* and *Discourse on Inequality*.

- *The Social Contract* is Rousseau's best-known work, although he was already famous before it was published.

Positioning

Jean-Jacques Rousseau's *The Social Contract* (1762) has been described as the culmination of Rousseau's political thought.[1] In 1750, Rousseau published his work *Discourse on the Arts and Sciences* in which he argued that "the sciences and arts tend to affect the character of both individuals and institutions,"[2] and that these disciplines corrupt humanity. In 1755, Rousseau published his *Discourse on Inequality*, in which he took a slightly different approach. Here he argued, "The first source of evil is inequality; from inequality arose riches … From riches are born luxury and idleness; from luxury arose the fine arts, and from idleness the sciences."[3]

Rousseau's claim was that inequality was a product of human action. People wish to position themselves above other people, and they create laws and the state in order to achieve this.[4] "Such political societies," he claimed, "based merely on power, could never make a moral claim to the allegiance of their members."[5] The purpose of *The Social Contract* was to provide an account of a "political system in

> ❝ Whenever the last trumpet shall sound, I will present myself before the sovereign judge with this book in my hand, and loudly proclaim, thus have I acted; these were my thoughts; such was I. ❞
>
> Jean-Jacques Rousseau, *The Confessions*

which all citizens would be treated as free and equal."[6] This would be a system that individuals would be committed to because it "would express their own will and promote the good of all."[7]

Integration

While it could be argued that there is coherence within Rousseau's political work, it would be very difficult to claim that his work had an overall direction: he was a prodigious writer who wrote on a vast number of topics. He wrote topics on music for the French writer Diderot's* *Encyclopédie** (his general encyclopedia), where he argued that music should inspire the passions.[8] His work Émile was his thesis on the philosophy of education, in which he set out his views on "how to raise a morally virtuous human being and citizen."[9]

In 1761, Rousseau published *Julie, or the New Heloise*—one of the most popular French novels in the eighteenth century.[10] Rousseau also wrote three autobiographical works: *The Confessions*, published posthumously in 1782, *Dialogues: Rousseau, Judge of Jean-Jacques* completed in 1776, and *Reveries of a Solitary Walker*, also published in 1782. Following the banning of *The Social Contract*, Rousseau believed that there was a conspiracy against him, and it is largely the case that "his autobiographical works are an attempt to defend himself against it."[11] The only consistent theme is that in almost everything Rousseau wrote he was a contrarian—he rejected the received opinions of the time and provided original arguments based on his own views and experiences.

Significance

The Social Contract is certainly Rousseau's "most comprehensive work of political philosophy."[12] But whether it is Rousseau's best work is a difficult question to answer. While it is regarded by many as his outstanding political work, the novel Émile, or On Education, also published in 1762, is also considered to be one of Rousseau's great works.[13]

Rousseau initially became a well-known figure thanks to his work in the field of music: "He was a much-admired composer and the author of a substantial and learned dictionary of music."[14] But it was his work *Discourse on the Sciences and Arts* (1750) that brought Rousseau to the attention of France's brightest minds: "The acclaim that immediately descended upon him from France's intellectual class was perhaps unprecedented not merely in Rousseau's own life but in his whole century."[15]

Rousseau went on to develop his reputation further with his 1752 opera *The Village Soothsayer*, a popular work that was even performed for the king.[16] By the time Rousseau published his *Discourse on Inequality*, he was already famous, and his article on political economy in the fifth edition of Diderot's *Encyclopédie* firmly established him as one the leading political theorists in Europe.[17]

Since his death in 1778, Rousseau has split opinion. For many British thinkers and politicians in the nineteenth century, for example, "Rousseau was an exemplar of dangerous continental extremism."[18] While this point of view is no longer widely held, Rousseau has the ability to arouse extreme reactions either in his favor or against him; as Christopher D. Wraight* states, "he tends to strike his readers either as a muddle-headed charlatan or a secular prophet of signal importance and vision."[19]

NOTES

1   Matthew Simpson, *Rousseau: A Guide for the Perplexed* (New York: Continuum, 2007), 22.

2   Simpson, *Rousseau*, 46.

3   Simpson, *Rousseau*, 52.

4   Simpson, *Rousseau*, 22.

5   Simpson, *Rousseau*, 22.

6   Simpson, *Rousseau*, 22.

7   Simpson, *Rousseau*, 22.

8   Christopher Bertram, *Routledge Philosophy Guidebook to Rousseau and the Social Contract* (London: Routledge, 2004), 12

9   James Delaney, *Starting with Rousseau* (New York: Continuum, 2009), 6.

10 Robert Wolker, *Rousseau: A Very Short Introduction* (Oxford: Oxford University Press, 2001), 15.

11 Delaney, *Starting with Rousseau*, 6.

12 Delaney, *Starting with Rousseau*, 6.

13 Christopher D. Wraight, *Rousseau's 'The Social Contract': A Reader's Guide* (New York: Continuum, 2008), 7.

14 Wolker, *Rousseau*, 1.

15 Simpson, *Rousseau*, 16.

16 Simpson, *Rousseau*, 17.

17 Simpson, *Rousseau*, 19.

18 Wraight, *Rousseau's 'The Social Contract'*, 120.

19 Wraight, *Rousseau's 'The Social Contract'*, 120.

SECTION 3
IMPACT

MODULE 9
THE FIRST RESPONSES

KEY POINTS

- Criticisms at the time *The Social Contract* was published focused on the lack of evidence for a social contract* ever taking place, the conditions under which a social contract could be entered into, and whether democracy* was compatible with liberty.

- Responses to these criticisms stated that the idea of the social contract should be seen as a thought experiment rather than a historical account.

- The work's reception was shaped by the French Revolution* and the events that followed.

Criticism

In a way, the timeline of the criticism of Jean-Jacques Rousseau's *The Social Contract* runs backward—the most important response to his ideas came before *The Social Contract* was published. In his 1748 essay *Of the Original Contract*, the Scottish philosopher David Hume* presented his critique of social contract theory: "Hume's objections," it has been said, "were so broad in scope that they posed problems for all contractualist theories, even one as sophisticated as Rousseau's."[1]

While Hume made a number of criticisms of the social contract tradition, it is possible to identify the most important arguments. The first problem is the fact that the theory "derives all political rights and obligations from a social contract, yet there never was such a contract in the history of the world."[2] If there never was such a social contract, why should anybody be "required to obey principles whose moral force, according to Rousseau, comes only from their being assented to"?[3]

❺❺ Hume, one of the great philosophers of the age, seemed not to warm to Rousseau's political philosophy at all, claiming that the belief that *The Social Contract* was of more interest than *Julie* was as absurd as the belief that Milton's* *Paradise Regained* was superior to *Paradise Lost.* ❻❻

Christopher D. Wraight,* *Rousseau's 'The Social Contract': A Reader's Guide*

Another criticism Hume puts forward relates to "the conditions under which the social contract is made."[4] The basic idea of Rousseau's argument concerning the social contract is that if people consent to be part of a society they are obligated to be bound by the rules of that society. This is only the case, however, if the conditions of agreement are free and fair, otherwise the consent is not genuine (this was also the central point of Rousseau's criticism of Hugo Grotius's* argument for a legitimate state). However, Rousseau also argues "there are no principles of obligation outside the social pact."[5] This makes it impossible to say whether or not the conditions under which the social contract was agreed to were fair.[6]

A final criticism comes from the Swiss philosopher and politician Benjamin Constant* in his 1816 speech *The Liberty of the Ancients Compared with that of the Moderns.* While Constant's argument is somewhat complex, it can be summarized as follows: because democracy requires "that the people be molded into citizen-machines it cannot coexist with broad individual freedom."[7] Constant's criticism effectively challenges Rousseau's argument that it is possible to live under a coercive* government and at the same time be truly free. He suggested that we must settle for "peaceful enjoyment and private independence."[8]

Responses

Although Rousseau did not respond directly to the criticisms above, we can read counterarguments in his work. Hume's first criticism focuses on the fact that there has never actually been a social contract. But Rousseau writes in *The Social Contract* that, while it is true that there are no actually existing examples, it does not matter for his overall theory, because the social contract is meant to be a conceptual tool, rather than a historical fact; as one commentator has put it, "the social contract is an ideal for society in light of which one can judge existing institutions."[9] The purpose of the concept of the social contract is not to exactly define what obligations and freedoms individuals will agree to; it is a thought experiment to assess whether current political arrangements allow people to live freely.

Hume's second objection is more difficult for Rousseau to deal with.[10] Hume suggests that there is no way to know whether the conditions for entering into a social contract are free and fair, because outside of the social contract individuals have no obligations to one another. Rousseau responds, "What is good and in conformity with order is such by the very nature of things and independent of human agreement. All justice comes from God."[11] What he means by this is that "the social contract must be made under free and fair terms, because those terms would be the ones consistent with the natural principles of justice."[12] In other words, humans have a natural tendency to be free and fair. But this contradicts another aspect of Rousseau's ideas; he also states in *The Social Contract* that there are no obligations in the state of nature:* "it is not clear he can make the argument that 'there are no natural duties and that all obligations are founded on the social pact.'"[13]

On the criticism from Benjamin Constant, which came after Rousseau's death, Rousseau's response might be that he and Constant simply thought about the trade-off between democracy and freedom differently; Rousseau was not as willing to give up on democracy in order to preserve individual liberty.[14] Rousseau's aim was to "reconcile a robust defence of individual rights with a plausible theory of sovereignty.*"[15] Added to this, Rousseau also contended that his system of direct democracy* enabled the people to ensure that they would not have to sacrifice their own liberty.

Conflict and Consensus

If neither Rousseau nor the critics he engaged with were able to reach an agreement, it is largely because of the nature of the topics under discussion. The debates focused on issues such as democracy or liberty, which are often referred to as "essentially contested concepts"*—they are ideas that it is very difficult to come to agreement on. While many people might agree that democracy is a preferable form of government, there will always be fundamental disagreement about what democracy actually is. For example, is representative democracy*—in which politicians represent the people who elected them—still rule by the people? Rousseau thinks it is not, but this is not a universal view. Whenever essentially contested concepts are discussed, it will be very difficult to reach a consensus; the very nature of these ideas suggests consensus is unlikely.

The debate concerning the validity of Rousseau's account of the social contract at the time of publication is largely separate from the later debates surrounding the work. Many of these later debates have focused on whether or not the arguments in *The Social Contract* could be used to justify totalitarianism*—a system of government in which the citizen is entirely subject to the state and the expense of their liberty. This shift in debate came about largely because of the events that unfolded during the French Revolution* (since many of those involved were inspired by his ideas), and after it (when an authoritarian* government, under which citizens were intrusively subject to government control, was established in France).

NOTES

1   Matthew Simpson, *Rousseau: A Guide for the Perplexed* (New York: Continuum, 2007), 94.

2   Simpson, *Rousseau*, 94.

3   Simpson, *Rousseau*, 95.

4   Simpson, *Rousseau*, 96.

5   Simpson, *Rousseau*, 97.

6   Simpson, *Rousseau*, 97.

7   Simpson, *Rousseau*, 102.

8   Simpson, *Rousseau*, 102.

9   Simpson, *Rousseau*, 96.

10   Simpson, *Rousseau*, 96.

11   Jean-Jacques Rousseau, *The Social Contract* (London: Penguin Classics, 1968), 80.

12   Simpson, *Rousseau*, 97.

13   Simpson, *Rousseau*, 98.

14   Simpson, *Rousseau*, 103.

15   Simpson, *Rousseau*, 103.

MODULE 10
THE EVOLVING DEBATE

KEY POINTS

- Rousseau's idea of the general will* in *The Social Contract* has been criticized for potentially paving the way for totalitarianism.*

- Many schools of thought have emerged from Rousseau's work; one of the most important is the cultural movement of Romanticism.*

- The US political philosopher John Rawls* was deeply influenced by Rousseau's work.

Uses and Problems

The French Revolution* began 27 years after the publication of Jean-Jacques Rousseau's *The Social Contract* and a decade after his death; many of the leaders of the Revolution "drew up their programs and constitutions in the fiery light of his philosophy."[1] Rousseau's reputation suffered when "the Revolution soured and gave birth, first to the Jacobin Terror,* then to Bonapartism,* and according to his critics, eventually to modern totalitarianism in general."[2] During the "Jacobin Terror," many thousands of people were executed in the name of ideological purity; "Bonapartism" is the name given to the authoritarian* political philosophy of the French emperor and dictator Napoleon Bonaparte.*

These historical events led thinkers such as the British political theorist Isaiah Berlin* to make the case that Rousseau's argument, and especially his use of the general will, could lead to totalitarianism.

According to this argument, the general will is "something abstract and ideal to be contrasted with the actual wants, desires and beliefs of

> **❝** Rousseau himself never advocated revolution, judged political uprisings worse than the disease they were intended to cure, and held little hope for the political salvation of mankind. **❞**
>
> Robert Wolker, *Rousseau: A Very Short Introduction*

the citizenry."[3] This means that the people have to be thought of as a single entity that acts only in the public interest. As sovereign,* power only belongs to the people as a whole; each individual is only relevant because they are a small part of this whole. According to Rousseau's critics, the individual as a single entity no longer truly exists, and if there are no longer any individuals then there can be no individual liberty under the general will. Each person must go along with the general will, and if they do not they will be forced to do so. Critics of the socialist* movements of the twentieth century, which argued for trade and industry to be held in common hands in order to achieve social equality, argue that this makes socialism a threat to "individual liberty and private property."[4]

It is interesting, however, that this criticism has come mainly from conservative* thinkers involved in the discipline of political thought. Many thinkers more associated with philosophy have taken the idea of the general will in a different direction. In contrast to the argument made by certain political thinkers that the general will is too idealistic, philosophers have argued that it is not idealistic enough.[5] This is the position taken by thinkers such as the German philosopher Immanuel Kant* and the US philosopher John Rawls. The Rousseau scholar Christopher Bertram* argues that each "has sought to make use of some notion derivative of the general will, but one purified of the imperfections of real people."[6]

Kant does this through the application of reason to morality; Rawls achieves this through his use of the "original position"* thought experiment, in which individuals are asked to put themselves in a position where they do not know anything about their own lives (their wealth, social status etc) and use this as the basis for deciding how society should be run; it is easier to imagine a society founded on principles of equality, for example, if one can imagine the possibility of living a life in poverty.

Schools of Thought

The Social Contract is one of the most influential works in the history of political thought and Rousseau "has been associated with almost every school of thought and political movement of Western modernity."[7]

Indeed, some specific schools of thought directly follow from Rousseau's ideas. While Rousseau is generally seen as an Enlightenment* thinker, "much of what Rousseau advocates is also significantly out of sympathy with the general direction of the Enlightenment."[8] As such he has also been associated with the school of thought of Romanticism.

Where the Enlightenment embraced reason, Romanticism involves "a privileged role for the emotions and a rejection of the rationalization of the natural world."[9] While what this involves precisely is somewhat difficult to define, the Romantics did argue that living a good life must involve living according to one's passions and "to revel in the full struggle and contradiction of the world seen through the prism of the emotions."[10] Romantic ideas were well expressed through literary works, by writers such as the English poets William Wordsworth* and Lord Byron.*[11] The most important of Rousseau's ideas for the Romantic movement was his "continual appreciation of the natural goodness of people and the usefulness of all their inherent drives."[12] *The Social Contract*, then, was an influential work for the Romantics.

In Current Scholarship

The most important modern thinker to have been inspired by Rousseau is John Rawls, one of the most influential philosophers of the twentieth century. In his work *A Theory of Justice*, Rawls attempts to answer a question very similar to the one that Rousseau starts with:[13] "What mechanism can we use to determine a universally binding set of fair principles of justice and governance, given that all of us have different individual desires, abilities and demands?"[14]

Rawls's solution to this problem has some similarities to the way Rousseau goes about answering it. Rawls also embraces a contractual approach[15] (an approach based on the idea of a social contract*), and his use of the "original position" is similar to Rousseau's use of the state of nature.*[16] The original position is used to ensure that the rules that people agree to be bound by are fair, since, according to the thought experiment, no one knows who they will be or their role in the imagined society. Under these conditions, Rawls argued, individuals are more likely to choose rules that are fair for everyone, and that guarantee that people have equal access to "fundamental rights and goods."[17]

Rawls explicitly acknowledges his debt to Rousseau, writing, "My aim is to present a conception of justice which generalizes and carries to a higher level of abstraction the familiar theory of the social contract as found, say, in Locke,* Rousseau and Kant."[18] In other words, he wants to take Rousseau's ideas even further.

NOTES

1   Robert Wolker, *Rousseau: A Very Short Introduction* (Oxford: Oxford University Press, 2001), 22.

2   Wolker, *Rousseau*, 22.

3   Christopher Bertram, *Routledge Philosophy Guidebook to Rousseau and the* Social Contract (London: Routledge, 2004), 191.

4   Bertram, *Routledge Philosophy GuideBook*, 191.

5   Bertram, *Routledge Philosophy GuideBook*, 191.

6   Bertram, *Routledge Philosophy GuideBook*, 191.

7   Tracy B. Strong, *Jean-Jacques Rousseau: The Politics of the Ordinary* (Lanham, MD: Rowman & Littlefield, 2002), 1.

8   Christopher D. Wraight, *Rousseau's 'The Social Contract': A Reader's Guide* (New York: Continuum, 2008), 126.

9   Wraight, *Rousseau's 'The Social Contract'*, 126.

10 Wraight, *Rousseau's 'The Social Contract'*, 126.

11 Wraight, *Rousseau's 'The Social Contract'*, 126.

12 Wraight, *Rousseau's 'The Social Contract'*, 127.

13 Wraight, *Rousseau's 'The Social Contract'*, 128.

14 Wraight, *Rousseau's 'The Social Contract'*, 128.

15 Wraight, *Rousseau's 'The Social Contract'*, 128.

16 Wraight, *Rousseau's 'The Social Contract'*, 128.

17 Wraight, *Rousseau's 'The Social Contract'*, 128.

18 John Rawls, *A Theory of Justice* (Cambridge, MA: Harvard University Press, 2009), 10.

MODULE 11
IMPACT AND INFLUENCE TODAY

KEY POINTS

- *The Social Contract* is viewed as one of the most important pieces of political thought ever published.

- The work encourages readers to think about the threat to human freedom posed by private interests, not just the state.

- Those that respond to this challenge emphasize that Rousseau's ideas can be used to justify significant reductions in the liberty of individuals.

Position

Jean-Jacques Rousseau's *The Social Contract* is not simply a text of great historical importance; it is a text that still continues "to help shape contemporary responses to problems of political right and equality."[1] There is no doubt that *The Social Contract* is a classic piece of work that has inspired an astonishing amount of debate. The reason for this is the fundamental nature of Rousseau's project—his aim to "find a state that managed to combine the authority necessary to coordinate the private activity of its constituent members without giving up the right of directing themselves."[2] In other words, Rousseau wanted to find a way that society could be both organized and free.

The question of how individuals can be free while being directed by a system of laws still endures. In the time since the work's publication, "the claim that the ideal state described and advocated there is a locus of individual freedom has come under sustained attack."[3] So it is difficult to say that there is a consensus view on *The Social Contract*. Critics claim that "the freedom allegedly enjoyed by the

> **❝** Despite the oddity of his life, Rousseau has remained at the forefront of our culture for a quarter of a millennium and the effects of his work continue to be felt. **❞**
>
> Christopher Bertram,* *Routledge Philosophy GuideBook to Rousseau and the* Social Contract

citizens [described in the book] is a fraud or sham, and … the real picture generated by Rousseau is one of totalitarianism.*"[4]

While *The Social Contract* is rarely involved directly in the political debates of today, ideas that it has inspired, such as those found in John Rawls's* *A Theory of Justice*, are still routinely used in contemporary debates about the nature of a fair society and what individuals owe one another.

Interaction

One of the most important aspects of Rousseau's work is that he thinks deeply about the role of the public interest.[5] This is important because *The Social Contract* sheds light on an area often ignored by other elements of political thought—how best can we make sure that private interests do not work against the common good?[6] Libertarians* (those who take the position that the state should interfere in the individual's life as little as possible) are particularly challenged by this point of view, tending to "see the world in terms of two relevant actors: the state and the individual, with the political task being to restrain the state's power over the individual."[7]

What the libertarian way of thinking ignores is that the state is not the only power that can limit the freedom of people. It is possible that people can have their freedom reduced by private individuals as well.[8] *The Social Contract* is a discussion of how a political system can be structured to avoid people being dominated by private interests.

Libertarians have tended not to respond to Rousseau directly, but to those inspired by Rousseau, most notably Rawls. Against Rawls's ideas, libertarian thinkers such as the US philosopher Robert Nozick* have argued that the only justifiable state that does not invalidate the rights of the individual is the minimal state,* where the role of the state is limited to upholding property rights and protecting people from aggression from others. Nozick puts this argument forward in his 1974 work *Anarchy, State and Utopia*.

The Continuing Debate

While *The Social Contract* is generally not debated fiercely in modern academia, some responses to the text are worth considering. Conservatives* have been fairly suspicious of Rousseau's system of thought, arguing that his ideas led directly to unnecessary violence during the French Revolution.* Thinkers such as the conservative Irish political theorist Edmund Burke* criticized Rousseau on these grounds. Burke referred to Rousseau as "the 'insane Socrates'* who had inspired a wholly destructive generation of men's moral constitution, and in whose memory the foundries of Paris were then casting their statutes, 'with the kettles of their poor and the bells of their churches.'"[9]

Thinkers on the left such as the American sociologist Daniel Bell* have also criticized Rousseau from a similar perspective. Bell argued that the demands of Rousseau's system of government ended up trampling the freedom of the individual: "The price of equality [in the *Social Contract*] is … that 'an individual can no longer claim anything'; he has no individual rights; 'his person and his whole power' are dissolved into the general will."[10] For Bell, this political system would inevitably result in a totalitarian* government, under whose rule each individual would have to sacrifice their own freedom for the general good.

NOTES

1   Christopher D. Wraight, *Rousseau's 'The Social Contract': A Reader's Guide* (New York: Continuum, 2008), 128.

2   Christopher Bertram, *Routledge Philosophy GuideBook to Rousseau and the* Social Contract (London: Routledge, 2004), 190.

3   Bertram, *Routledge Philosophy GuideBook*, 190.

4   Bertram, *Routledge Philosophy GuideBook*, 190.

5   Bertram, *Routledge Philosophy GuideBook*, 203.

6   Bertram, *Routledge Philosophy GuideBook*, 203.

7   Bertram, *Routledge Philosophy GuideBook*, 203.

8   Bertram, *Routledge Philosophy GuideBook*, 203.

9   Robert Wolker, *Rousseau: A Very Short Introduction* (Oxford: Oxford University Press, 2001), 98.

10 David Lay Williams, *Rousseau's* Social Contract*: An Introduction* (Cambridge: Cambridge University Press: 2014), 2.

MODULE 12
WHERE NEXT?

KEY POINTS

- *The Social Contract* is likely to remain an important piece of work for many years to come.

- Thanks to its important role in social contract* theory and the related questions The Social Contract attempts to answer, it will continue to have an impact on anyone using this framework to understand how societies work.

- *The Social Contract* is deeply influential as an essential resource for thinking about the legitimacy of political systems.

Potential

Readers are almost certain to regard Jean-Jacques Rousseau's *The Social Contract* as a classic for a long time to come. It has been considered one of the most important pieces in Western political thought for the last 250 years and there is little reason to suppose that this view will change. This is especially the case given the influence Rousseau has had on thinkers such as John Rawls,* an American philosopher whose work *A Theory of Justice* is central to many of the continuing debates within political philosophy.

Contemporary thinkers still find themselves addressing problems similar to those that Rousseau was discussing over two centuries ago; many of the responses made to Rousseau's argument, then, also remain relevant. So while *The Social Contract* is not necessarily at the center of contemporary political debates, it has provided many of the foundations on which contemporary political debate takes place. Rousseau raised important questions concerning how the state can

❝ We remain in the Romantic cycle initiated by Rousseau: liberal idealism* canceled by violence, barbarism, disillusionment and cynicism. ❞

Camille Paglia, *Sexual Personae*

enhance rather than diminish personal freedom—a question just as relevant today as it was when Rousseau posed it.

Future Directions

Given the significant and wide-ranging influence *The Social Contract* has had on a number of disciplines inside Western political thought, it is difficult to identify any particular thinkers as working specifically in Rousseau's tradition. The most fruitful way to think about those continuing Rousseau's project is to consider those working inside the social contract tradition such as John Rawls; while Rawls died over a decade ago, his work is still hugely important and continues to be hotly debated. It would not be a stretch to say that any current political philosopher is working within the framework set out by Rawls.

Another significant contemporary social contract theorist is the Canadian American thinker David Gauthier,* whose work *Morals by Agreement* was published in 1986. Gautier follows in the footsteps of Rousseau and other social contract theorists such as Thomas Hobbes.* He argues that the conditions of morality must be based on an agreement undertaken by individuals, and uses the insights of rational choice theory* to demonstrate that cooperation between individuals is possible and beneficial when it comes to making decisions about morality. Rational choice theory is a way of understanding economic and social action starting with the idea that individuals have preferences and will act consistently and rationally in order to achieve them.

In France, Rousseau's account of the social contract has been applied to the debate concerning multiculturalism*—the existence of parallel cultures inside a single state—and immigration. It has been suggested that new entrants into a society should integrate into the practices of that society through adhering to a social contract such as the one proposed by Rousseau.[1] But this has raised questions concerning the nature of the social contract that a new member of a society should be expected to sign up to. It has been suggested that asking immigrants to subscribe to the social contract and therefore the general will* forces them to assimilate (to be incorporated) into the general society and culture, whereas many people might prefer to keep hold of their own cultural or individual identity. On the other side of the argument, it is claimed that if newly arrived members of a society do not submit to the general will, this will create social friction.

Summary

Students should continue to read Rousseau's *The Social Contract* because of the importance of the question that Rousseau addresses: What are the conditions for legitimate government? *The Social Contract* is one of the most fiercely debated and influential pieces of political philosophy in the history of Western political thought.

We can attribute the work's notable influence to Rousseau's status as one of only a few thinkers who tries "to think through what is needed if individuals are to escape becoming subject to the private wills of other individuals."[2] In other words, Rousseau thinks about how a society can avoid one person's freedom becoming another person's lack of freedom. Part of the work's continuing appeal is that it is a mixed bag: Rousseau's answers range from genius to indecipherable, meaning that that there is a tremendous amount of scope to debate and discuss the ideas he puts forward. As the Rousseau scholar Christopher Bertram* notes, Rousseau is significant in that "he squarely addresses faults in political culture and institutions that are plainly still with us and the *Social Contract* remains an indispensable resource in thinking about political power, legitimacy and freedom."[3]

For any student interested in the history of political thought, in political thought today, and insights into human nature, *The Social Contract* is invaluable reading.[4]

NOTES

1 Daniel Brunstetter, "Rousseau and the Tensions of France's *Contrat d'Accueil et d'Intégration*," *Journal of Political Ideologies* 17, no. 1 (2012): 1.

2 Christopher Bertram, *Routledge Philosophy GuideBook to Rousseau and the Social Contract* (London: Routledge, 2004), 203.

3 Bertram, *Routledge Philosophy GuideBook*, 203.

4 Christopher D. Wraight, *Rousseau's 'The Social Contract': A Reader's Guide* (New York: Continuum, 2008), 128.

GLOSSARY

GLOSSARY OF TERMS

Absolute monarchy: a type of government in which the monarch has complete and total power. There are no checks upon the power of the monarch and they are free to act however they wish in relation to the people and matters of state.

Authoritarian government: a form of government that involves a significant amount of control of individuals by the state. A dictator usually controls an authoritarian government.

Autonomy: in political philosophy, a term referring to one's ability to live the life one wants to live.

Bonapartism: the ideology held by Napoleon Bonaparte, the emperor of France at the start of the nineteenth century. The ideology involved support for an authoritarian military government.

Capitalism: a social and economic system, dominant in the West (and increasingly throughout the developing world), in which trade and industry are held in private hands and conducted for the sake of private profit.

Coercion: when used in political philosophy, this refers to the use of force, or other punishments, to make an individual act in a particular way. Coercion can be both legitimate (fair) and illegitimate (unfair).

Conservatism: traditionally, a system of political thought that rejects ideology and rationalism and is defined by a suspicion of state power and a desire for small changes in place of big ideas—although this is not necessarily the case today.

Covenant: an alternative term for an agreement, or a contract.

Democracy: a system of government in which power is held in the hands of the people; modern democratic governments are usually formed by the election of representatives.

Direct democracy: a form of democracy that involves each person within a society voting on an issue. It is most associated with the form of democracy practiced in ancient Athens. In modern democracies, referendums (in which everyone can vote on a single issue) are forms of direct democracy.

Divine right of kings: a doctrine that supports the legitimacy of monarchs. It suggests that God chooses monarchs to rule and this is where their legitimacy comes from. As such they cannot be held accountable for their actions by nondivine institutions such as parliament.

*Encyclopédie***:** a general encyclopedia edited by the French writer Denis Diderot published between 1751 and 1772. Diderot wanted to change the way that people thought and to provide a tool for secular (nonreligious) education. The work was the first encyclopedia to feature contributions from a range of authors and is considered one of the major works of the Enlightenment.

Enlightenment: a cultural movement current in Western Europe between the mid-seventeenth century and the late eighteenth century. The Enlightenment was characterized by advances in science, philosophy, and political thought, and sought to move away from the religious and spiritual beliefs of the medieval world view.

Essentially contested concepts: ideas that have a wide variety of legitimate meanings, such as "fairness"; while many people would probably agree that social institutions should be fair, there is little agreement about what makes something fair or unfair.

Executive: the branch of government that ensures that laws passed by the legislator are obeyed; its role is to enforce the law.

Feudalism: a social, political, and economic system common in Europe between the fifth and seventeenth centuries. The feudal system involved allowing the use of land to grow food and live, in exchange for labor. Landowning lords had full control over the people who worked for them.

French Revolution: a revolutionary movement that took place between 1789 and 1799. It involved the removal of the ruling monarchy and the establishment of a republic, and was inspired by the idea that the people should rule. It has been criticized for the violence it prompted.

General will: a term Rousseau used to describe rule by the people in the interest of the community as a whole rather than in the interest of particular individuals.

Industrial Revolution: the period of economic transformation that came about through the adoption of new manufacturing processes; the Industrial Revolution started in the United Kingdom in the mid-eighteenth century and then spread to Western Europe over the next one hundred years.

Jacobin Terror: also known as "The Terror," this was a period of sustained violence and bloodshed following the French Revolution during which many people suspected of being against the Revolution were executed (often by guillotine). It is estimated around 40,000 people were executed in the name of the Revolution.

Lawgiver: a term used by Rousseau to describe the entity that guides the people to ensure that their decisions are in accordance with the general will.

Legislature: the branch of government concerned with the drafting, debating, and passing of laws.

Liberal idealism: the belief that people are essentially good and that

progress is possible through mutual cooperation. It also holds that corrupt political institutions are the main cause of negative behavior by individuals.

Liberalism: a form of government emphasizing the role of individual liberty. The term has different connotations in the fields of politics, economics, and international relations.

Libertarianism: a political ideology that is committed to individual liberty as its highest concern. Libertarians argue that the state is coercive and that in order to ensure that people are as free as possible the state should interfere in the lives as people as little as possible.

Metaphysics: the branch of philosophy dealing with fundamental questions of existence.

Minimal state: a term used to describe a state that only enforces property rights and contracts, and prevents aggression against individuals. The minimal state (also called the "night watchman" state) is favored by many libertarians.

Monarchy: a type of government where the monarch is sovereign—holding ultimate power. In practice, monarchies differ in terms of how much power the monarch actually holds, from an absolute monarchy (in which the monarch's word is law) to a constitutional monarchy (where the power of the monarchy is checked by democratic institutions).

Multiculturalism: in a basic sense, a term describing the existence of a number of different cultures within a single society. Multiculturalism as a political project tends to involve polices that aim at maintaining the distinctiveness of different cultures within a single society.

Original position: a name given to a thought experiment conducted by the US philosopher John Rawls in his work *A Theory of Justice.* The thought experiment involves individuals putting themselves in the "original position," a position where they do not know anything about where they might be placed (their status, wealth etc) in an imagined political and social system, and using this as the basis for deciding how a society should be governed in a fair way.

Popular sovereignty: the idea that the authority of a ruler or the state comes from the fact that the individuals that make up society have given their consent to be governed, meaning that the people themselves are the source of all political power; if they withdraw their consent the authority of the ruler or state is no longer legitimate.

Rational choice theory: a way of understanding economic and social action. The theory starts with the idea that individuals have preferences and will act consistently and rationally in order to achieve these preferences.

Representative democracy: a form of democracy that involves people within a society voting for a representative who will then make decisions on their behalf. Representative democracy is the most common form of democratic government.

Republic: a system of government in which sovereignty resides with the people rather than with a monarch and elected officials make decisions. Sometimes the term republic is used to describe any sovereign state that does not have a monarch, regardless of whether they have free elections or not.

Republic of Venice: a state that encompassed most of modern north-eastern Italy. It existed from 697 to 1797 and was powerful in both military and economic terms. Its government was made up of a head of state (the Doge), an aristocracy that formed the senate, and a democracy of major families that made up the council.

Roman Catholicism: a tradition within the Christian Church that dates back 2000 years. It is the largest of all the Christian religious traditions with over 1.2 billion followers worldwide.

Romanticism: a literary and artistic movement that came out of the political turmoil following the French Revolution and the social change after the Industrial Revolution. Romanticism emphasized the role of emotions and rejected the use of reason in political thought.

Social contract: a term given to the idea that people's political obligations are formed through an agreement made by the members of a society. Thinkers such as the political theorists John Locke, Thomas Hobbes, and Jean-Jacques Rousseau have all proposed some form of social contract theory.

Socialism: a school of political thought that stresses the importance of equality, achieved through democratic control of the means of production.

Sovereign: the element of government from which the ultimate decision power flows. In Rousseau's thought the sovereign is the people as a collective group, guided by the general will.

Sovereignty: the right of a particular individual or group to govern and assert authority over others. The sovereign is the party that has responsibility for governing, or is responsible for giving their consent to be governed, and no other parties may interfere in this.

State of nature: a concept that describes a hypothetical situation before societies and the state came into existence, often assumed to be chaotic and violent. It is often used in arguments to justify the existence of the state, as life under the state is thought to be preferable to life in the state of nature.

Totalitarianism: a system of government where there are no effective limits on the authority of the government. It is often associated with significant reductions of individual liberty as the state attempts to control many aspects of people's lives.

Utopian: a term used to describe an ideal or perfect society. Utopian can be used negatively, to suggest that while an idea might work in theory it is undermined by the fact it can never actually be achieved.

PEOPLE MENTIONED IN THE TEXT

Aristotle (384–322 B.C.E.) was an ancient Greek philosopher and a student of the influential philosopher Plato. He wrote on a wide range of subjects including ethics, physics, and politics, and is credited with being the first scientist in history.

Daniel Bell (1919–2011) was an American sociologist who worked at Harvard University. His work focused on the inherent problems in the capitalist system and he is best known for *The Cultural Contradictions of Capitalism* (1976).

Isaiah Berlin (1909–97) was a British political theorist and philosopher. He was one of the most preeminent thinkers of his generation and was best known for his work *Two Concepts of Liberty* (1958).

Christopher Bertram (b. 1958) is professor of social and political philosophy at the Department of Philosophy, University of Bristol. His main research interests include Rousseau, modern social contract theory, and theories of justice.

Napoleon Bonaparte (1769–1821) was a French military and political leader from the island of Corsica. His rise to power following the French Revolution changed the face of Europe forever and instigated a period of almost continuous war between 1803 and 1815 that involved every major European power.

Edmund Burke (1729–97) was an Irish political thinker and a member of the British parliament. He is most famous for his work criticizing the French Revolution, *Reflections on the Revolution in France* (1790).

Lord Byron (1788–1824) was an English poet, and one of the most influential members of the Romantic movement. He was known for living a life of excess, building up large debts and having numerous love affairs.

Benjamin Constant (1767–1830) was a Swiss journalist, politician, and philosopher who became one of France's foremost writers. He was deeply opposed to the concept of revolution and a great advocate of freedom and privacy.

James Delaney is an associate professor in philosophy at Niagara University. His research interests include Rousseau and personal identity.

Denis Diderot (1713–84) was a French philosopher who played a crucial role in the development of the Enlightenment. He is best known as the editor of *Encyclopédie* (his general encyclopedia).

David Gauthier (b. 1932) is a Canadian American political philosopher best known for his work in social contract theory. His most significant work is *Morals by Agreement* (1986).

Hugo Grotius (1583–1645) was a Dutch political philosopher. His work was one of the first attempts to establish the concept of international law, which he based on the theory of natural law.

Thomas Hobbes (1588–1679) was an English political philosopher, noted for his influential work *Leviathan* (1651), exploring social contract theory, liberty, and the nature of sovereignty.

David Hume (1711–76) was a Scottish philosopher, economist, and historian. He is widely regarded as one of the most important philosophers in history and is best known for his skepticism and radical empiricism.

Immanuel Kant (1724–1804) was a German philosopher and is regarded as the father of modern philosophy. He is best known for the view that reason is the foundation of all morality.

John Locke (1632–1704) was an English philosopher and a crucial figure in the development of the Enlightenment. He wrote on issues such as epistemology (the theory of knowledge) and political philosophy. His social contract theory was particularly influential.

Louis XIV of France (1638–1715) was a French monarch noted for his decadent lifestyle and his autocratic (despotic) style of ruling. He was king for 72 years, making him the longest serving monarch in European history.

Niccolò Machiavelli (1469–1527) was an Italian philosopher and politician who lived in Florence. He is most famous for *The Prince* (1513) in which he sets out how a leader can effectively rule.

John Milton (1608–74) was an English poet and historian, considered one the most important authors in English history. He is best known for his epic poem *Paradise Lost* (1667).

Baron de Montesquieu (1689–1755) was a French Enlightenment philosopher. His most famous idea is that of the separation of powers, which he saw as a way of avoiding despotism or dictatorship. The separation of powers involves political authority being split between an executive, a legislature, and a judiciary.

Robert Nozick (1938–2002) was an influential American philosopher. He is most famous for his libertarian critique of John Rawls's *A Theory of Justice*. However, he also published important works in decision theory and epistemology.

Plato (c. 428–347 B.C.E.) was an ancient Greek philosopher and mathematician. Credited as being one of the founders of Western philosophy, his most famous work is *Republic*.

John Rawls (1921–2002) was an American political philosopher and one of the most influential thinkers of the twentieth century. He is most famous for his work *A Theory of Justice* (1971).

Adam Smith (1723–90) was a Scottish economist and moral philosopher. He is most famous for his work *The Wealth of Nations* (1776), which earned him his reputation as the father of modern economics.

Socrates (470/469–399 B.C.E.) was an ancient Greek philosopher who is credited with having an enormous impact on the development of Western philosophy and culture. He was the teacher of Plato and came into conflict with the Athenian authorities for his radical views. He was put to death at the age of 70 for the crimes of impiety and the corruption of the youth of Athens.

Voltaire (1694–1778) was the pen name of François-Marie Arouet. Voltaire was a key figure of the Enlightenment period and was well known for his attacks on the power of the monarchy and the Church. He supported freedom of expression and freedom of religion.

Madame de Warens (1699–1762) was Rousseau's teacher, benefactor, and lover. Originally a Swiss Protestant, she converted to

Roman Catholicism in 1726, then annulled her marriage. She met Rousseau in 1728 and he describes his relationship with her in his work *The Confessions*.

David Lay Williams is a professor of political science at DePaul University. His research interests include the history of political thought and Rousseau's political thought.

William Wordsworth (1770–1850) was an English poet who wrote in the Romantic tradition. He was deeply influenced by the French Revolution, through which he gained a deep affinity with the troubles of working-class people.

Christopher D. Wraight has a PhD in philosophy from the University of Birmingham in the United Kingdom. He currently teaches with the Royal Institute of Philosophy.

WORKS CITED

WORKS CITED

Adams, Ian, and Robert W. Dyson. *Fifty Major Political Thinkers*. New York: Routledge, 2007.

Bertram, Christopher. *Routledge Philosophy GuideBook to Rousseau and the* Social Contract. London: Routledge, 2004.

Brunstetter, Daniel. "Rousseau and the Tensions of France's *Contrat d'Accueil et d'Intégration*." *Journal of Political Ideologies* 17, no. 1 (2012): 107–26.

Delaney, James. *Starting with Rousseau*. New York: Continuum, 2009.

Friend, Celeste. "Social Contract Theory." *Internet Encyclopaedia of Philosophy*, 2004. Accessed January 3, 2016. http://www.iep.utm.edu/soc-cont/.

Gaus, Gerald F., and Fred D'Agostino. *The Routledge Companion to Social and Political Philosophy*. New York: Routledge, 2013.

Hobbes, Thomas. *Leviathan*. Oxford: Oxford University Press, 1996.

Martin, Kingsley. *French Liberal Thought in the Eighteenth Century: A Study of Political Ideas from Bayle to Condorcet*. London: Turnstile Press, 1954.

Paglia, Camille. *Sexual Personae: Art and Decadence from Nefertiti to Emily Dickinson*. New Haven, CT: Yale University Press, 1990.

Rawls, John. *A Theory of Justice*. Cambridge, MA: Harvard University Press: 2009.

Rosenfeld, Michael. *Constitutionalism, Identity, Difference, and Legitimacy: Theoretical Perspectives*. Durham, NC: Duke University Press, 1994.

Rousseau, Jean-Jacques. *The Basic Political Writings*. Translated and edited by Donald A. Cress. Indianapolis, IN: Hackett Publishing, 2012.

The Confessions. London: Penguin Classics, 1953.

The Social Contract. London: Penguin Classics, 1968.

Simpson, Matthew. *Rousseau: A Guide for the Perplexed*. New York: Continuum, 2007.

Strong, Tracy B. *Jean-Jacques Rousseau: The Politics of the Ordinary*. Lanham, MD: Rowman & Littlefield, 2002.

Williams, David Lay. *Rousseau's* Social Contract*: An Introduction*. Cambridge: Cambridge University Press, 2014.

Wolker, Robert. *Rousseau: A Very Short Introduction*. Oxford: Oxford University Press, 2001.

Worthington, Daryl. "Rousseau's *The Social Contract*." *NewHistorian*, November 7, 2014. Accessed January 3, 2016. http://www.newmhistorian.com/rousseaus-social-contract/1972/.

Wraight, Christopher D. *Rousseau's 'The Social Contract': A Reader's Guide*. New York: Continuum, 2008.

THE MACAT LIBRARY
BY DISCIPLINE

AFRICANA STUDIES

Chinua Achebe's *An Image of Africa: Racism in Conrad's Heart of Darkness*
W. E. B. Du Bois's *The Souls of Black Folk*
Zora Neale Huston's *Characteristics of Negro Expression*
Martin Luther King Jr's *Why We Can't Wait*
Toni Morrison's *Playing in the Dark: Whiteness in the American Literary Imagination*

ANTHROPOLOGY

Arjun Appadurai's *Modernity at Large: Cultural Dimensions of Globalisation*
Philippe Ariès's *Centuries of Childhood*
Franz Boas's *Race, Language and Culture*
Kim Chan & Renée Mauborgne's *Blue Ocean Strategy*
Jared Diamond's *Guns, Germs & Steel: the Fate of Human Societies*
Jared Diamond's *Collapse: How Societies Choose to Fail or Survive*
E. E. Evans-Pritchard's *Witchcraft, Oracles and Magic Among the Azande*
James Ferguson's *The Anti-Politics Machine*
Clifford Geertz's *The Interpretation of Cultures*
David Graeber's *Debt: the First 5000 Years*
Karen Ho's *Liquidated: An Ethnography of Wall Street*
Geert Hofstede's *Culture's Consequences: Comparing Values, Behaviors, Institutes and Organizations across Nations*
Claude Lévi-Strauss's *Structural Anthropology*
Jay Macleod's *Ain't No Makin' It: Aspirations and Attainment in a Low-Income Neighborhood*
Saba Mahmood's *The Politics of Piety: The Islamic Revival and the Feminist Subject*
Marcel Mauss's *The Gift*

BUSINESS

Jean Lave & Etienne Wenger's *Situated Learning*
Theodore Levitt's *Marketing Myopia*
Burton G. Malkiel's *A Random Walk Down Wall Street*
Douglas McGregor's *The Human Side of Enterprise*
Michael Porter's *Competitive Strategy: Creating and Sustaining Superior Performance*
John Kotter's *Leading Change*
C. K. Prahalad & Gary Hamel's *The Core Competence of the Corporation*

CRIMINOLOGY

Michelle Alexander's *The New Jim Crow: Mass Incarceration in the Age of Colorblindness*
Michael R. Gottfredson & Travis Hirschi's *A General Theory of Crime*
Richard Herrnstein & Charles A. Murray's *The Bell Curve: Intelligence and Class Structure in American Life*
Elizabeth Loftus's *Eyewitness Testimony*
Jay Macleod's *Ain't No Makin' It: Aspirations and Attainment in a Low-Income Neighborhood*
Philip Zimbardo's *The Lucifer Effect*

ECONOMICS

Janet Abu-Lughod's *Before European Hegemony*
Ha-Joon Chang's *Kicking Away the Ladder*
David Brion Davis's *The Problem of Slavery in the Age of Revolution*
Milton Friedman's *The Role of Monetary Policy*
Milton Friedman's *Capitalism and Freedom*
David Graeber's *Debt: the First 5000 Years*
Friedrich Hayek's *The Road to Serfdom*
Karen Ho's *Liquidated: An Ethnography of Wall Street*

The Macat Library By Discipline

John Maynard Keynes's *The General Theory of Employment, Interest and Money*
Charles P. Kindleberger's *Manias, Panics and Crashes*
Robert Lucas's *Why Doesn't Capital Flow from Rich to Poor Countries?*
Burton G. Malkiel's *A Random Walk Down Wall Street*
Thomas Robert Malthus's *An Essay on the Principle of Population*
Karl Marx's *Capital*
Thomas Piketty's *Capital in the Twenty-First Century*
Amartya Sen's *Development as Freedom*
Adam Smith's *The Wealth of Nations*
Nassim Nicholas Taleb's *The Black Swan: The Impact of the Highly Improbable*
Amos Tversky's & Daniel Kahneman's *Judgment under Uncertainty: Heuristics and Biases*
Mahbub Ul Haq's *Reflections on Human Development*
Max Weber's *The Protestant Ethic and the Spirit of Capitalism*

FEMINISM AND GENDER STUDIES

Judith Butler's *Gender Trouble*
Simone De Beauvoir's *The Second Sex*
Michel Foucault's *History of Sexuality*
Betty Friedan's *The Feminine Mystique*
Saba Mahmood's *The Politics of Piety: The Islamic Revival and the Feminist Subject*
Joan Wallach Scott's *Gender and the Politics of History*
Mary Wollstonecraft's *A Vindication of the Rights of Woman*
Virginia Woolf's *A Room of One's Own*

GEOGRAPHY

The Brundtland Report's *Our Common Future*
Rachel Carson's *Silent Spring*
Charles Darwin's *On the Origin of Species*
James Ferguson's *The Anti-Politics Machine*
Jane Jacobs's *The Death and Life of Great American Cities*
James Lovelock's *Gaia: A New Look at Life on Earth*
Amartya Sen's *Development as Freedom*
Mathis Wackernagel & William Rees's *Our Ecological Footprint*

HISTORY

Janet Abu-Lughod's *Before European Hegemony*
Benedict Anderson's *Imagined Communities*
Bernard Bailyn's *The Ideological Origins of the American Revolution*
Hanna Batatu's *The Old Social Classes And The Revolutionary Movements Of Iraq*
Christopher Browning's *Ordinary Men: Reserve Police Batallion 101 and the Final Solution in Poland*
Edmund Burke's *Reflections on the Revolution in France*
William Cronon's *Nature's Metropolis: Chicago And The Great West*
Alfred W. Crosby's *The Columbian Exchange*
Hamid Dabashi's *Iran: A People Interrupted*
David Brion Davis's *The Problem of Slavery in the Age of Revolution*
Nathalie Zemon Davis's *The Return of Martin Guerre*
Jared Diamond's *Guns, Germs & Steel: the Fate of Human Societies*
Frank Dikotter's *Mao's Great Famine*
John W Dower's *War Without Mercy: Race And Power In The Pacific War*
W. E. B. Du Bois's *The Souls of Black Folk*
Richard J. Evans's *In Defence of History*
Lucien Febvre's *The Problem of Unbelief in the 16th Century*
Sheila Fitzpatrick's *Everyday Stalinism*

Eric Foner's *Reconstruction: America's Unfinished Revolution, 1863-1877*
Michel Foucault's *Discipline and Punish*
Michel Foucault's *History of Sexuality*
Francis Fukuyama's *The End of History and the Last Man*
John Lewis Gaddis's *We Now Know: Rethinking Cold War History*
Ernest Gellner's *Nations and Nationalism*
Eugene Genovese's *Roll, Jordan, Roll: The World the Slaves Made*
Carlo Ginzburg's *The Night Battles*
Daniel Goldhagen's *Hitler's Willing Executioners*
Jack Goldstone's *Revolution and Rebellion in the Early Modern World*
Antonio Gramsci's *The Prison Notebooks*
Alexander Hamilton, John Jay & James Madison's *The Federalist Papers*
Christopher Hill's *The World Turned Upside Down*
Carole Hillenbrand's *The Crusades: Islamic Perspectives*
Thomas Hobbes's *Leviathan*
Eric Hobsbawm's *The Age Of Revolution*
John A. Hobson's *Imperialism: A Study*
Albert Hourani's *History of the Arab Peoples*
Samuel P. Huntington's *The Clash of Civilizations and the Remaking of World Order*
C. L. R. James's *The Black Jacobins*
Tony Judt's *Postwar: A History of Europe Since 1945*
Ernst Kantorowicz's *The King's Two Bodies: A Study in Medieval Political Theology*
Paul Kennedy's *The Rise and Fall of the Great Powers*
Ian Kershaw's *The "Hitler Myth": Image and Reality in the Third Reich*
John Maynard Keynes's *The General Theory of Employment, Interest and Money*
Charles P. Kindleberger's *Manias, Panics and Crashes*
Martin Luther King Jr's *Why We Can't Wait*
Henry Kissinger's *World Order: Reflections on the Character of Nations and the Course of History*
Thomas Kuhn's *The Structure of Scientific Revolutions*
Georges Lefebvre's *The Coming of the French Revolution*
John Locke's *Two Treatises of Government*
Niccolò Machiavelli's *The Prince*
Thomas Robert Malthus's *An Essay on the Principle of Population*
Mahmood Mamdani's *Citizen and Subject: Contemporary Africa And The Legacy Of Late Colonialism*
Karl Marx's *Capital*
Stanley Milgram's *Obedience to Authority*
John Stuart Mill's *On Liberty*
Thomas Paine's *Common Sense*
Thomas Paine's *Rights of Man*
Geoffrey Parker's *Global Crisis: War, Climate Change and Catastrophe in the Seventeenth Century*
Jonathan Riley-Smith's *The First Crusade and the Idea of Crusading*
Jean-Jacques Rousseau's *The Social Contract*
Joan Wallach Scott's *Gender and the Politics of History*
Theda Skocpol's *States and Social Revolutions*
Adam Smith's *The Wealth of Nations*
Timothy Snyder's *Bloodlands: Europe Between Hitler and Stalin*
Sun Tzu's *The Art of War*
Keith Thomas's *Religion and the Decline of Magic*
Thucydides's *The History of the Peloponnesian War*
Frederick Jackson Turner's *The Significance of the Frontier in American History*
Odd Arne Westad's *The Global Cold War: Third World Interventions And The Making Of Our Times*

LITERATURE

Chinua Achebe's *An Image of Africa: Racism in Conrad's Heart of Darkness*
Roland Barthes's *Mythologies*
Homi K. Bhabha's *The Location of Culture*
Judith Butler's *Gender Trouble*
Simone De Beauvoir's *The Second Sex*
Ferdinand De Saussure's *Course in General Linguistics*
T. S. Eliot's *The Sacred Wood: Essays on Poetry and Criticism*
Zora Neale Huston's *Characteristics of Negro Expression*
Toni Morrison's *Playing in the Dark: Whiteness in the American Literary Imagination*
Edward Said's *Orientalism*
Gayatri Chakravorty Spivak's *Can the Subaltern Speak?*
Mary Wollstonecraft's *A Vindication of the Rights of Women*
Virginia Woolf's *A Room of One's Own*

PHILOSOPHY

Elizabeth Anscombe's *Modern Moral Philosophy*
Hannah Arendt's *The Human Condition*
Aristotle's *Metaphysics*
Aristotle's *Nicomachean Ethics*
Edmund Gettier's *Is Justified True Belief Knowledge?*
Georg Wilhelm Friedrich Hegel's *Phenomenology of Spirit*
David Hume's *Dialogues Concerning Natural Religion*
David Hume's *The Enquiry for Human Understanding*
Immanuel Kant's *Religion within the Boundaries of Mere Reason*
Immanuel Kant's *Critique of Pure Reason*
Søren Kierkegaard's *The Sickness Unto Death*
Søren Kierkegaard's *Fear and Trembling*
C. S. Lewis's *The Abolition of Man*
Alasdair MacIntyre's *After Virtue*
Marcus Aurelius's *Meditations*
Friedrich Nietzsche's *On the Genealogy of Morality*
Friedrich Nietzsche's *Beyond Good and Evil*
Plato's *Republic*
Plato's *Symposium*
Jean-Jacques Rousseau's *The Social Contract*
Gilbert Ryle's *The Concept of Mind*
Baruch Spinoza's *Ethics*
Sun Tzu's *The Art of War*
Ludwig Wittgenstein's *Philosophical Investigations*

POLITICS

Benedict Anderson's *Imagined Communities*
Aristotle's *Politics*
Bernard Bailyn's *The Ideological Origins of the American Revolution*
Edmund Burke's *Reflections on the Revolution in France*
John C. Calhoun's *A Disquisition on Government*
Ha-Joon Chang's *Kicking Away the Ladder*
Hamid Dabashi's *Iran: A People Interrupted*
Hamid Dabashi's *Theology of Discontent: The Ideological Foundation of the Islamic Revolution in Iran*
Robert Dahl's *Democracy and its Critics*
Robert Dahl's *Who Governs?*
David Brion Davis's *The Problem of Slavery in the Age of Revolution*

Alexis De Tocqueville's *Democracy in America*
James Ferguson's *The Anti-Politics Machine*
Frank Dikotter's *Mao's Great Famine*
Sheila Fitzpatrick's *Everyday Stalinism*
Eric Foner's *Reconstruction: America's Unfinished Revolution, 1863-1877*
Milton Friedman's *Capitalism and Freedom*
Francis Fukuyama's *The End of History and the Last Man*
John Lewis Gaddis's *We Now Know: Rethinking Cold War History*
Ernest Gellner's *Nations and Nationalism*
David Graeber's *Debt: the First 5000 Years*
Antonio Gramsci's *The Prison Notebooks*
Alexander Hamilton, John Jay & James Madison's *The Federalist Papers*
Friedrich Hayek's *The Road to Serfdom*
Christopher Hill's *The World Turned Upside Down*
Thomas Hobbes's *Leviathan*
John A. Hobson's *Imperialism: A Study*
Samuel P. Huntington's *The Clash of Civilizations and the Remaking of World Order*
Tony Judt's *Postwar: A History of Europe Since 1945*
David C. Kang's *China Rising: Peace, Power and Order in East Asia*
Paul Kennedy's *The Rise and Fall of Great Powers*
Robert Keohane's *After Hegemony*
Martin Luther King Jr.'s *Why We Can't Wait*
Henry Kissinger's *World Order: Reflections on the Character of Nations and the Course of History*
John Locke's *Two Treatises of Government*
Niccolò Machiavelli's *The Prince*
Thomas Robert Malthus's *An Essay on the Principle of Population*
Mahmood Mamdani's *Citizen and Subject: Contemporary Africa And The Legacy Of Late Colonialism*
Karl Marx's *Capital*
John Stuart Mill's *On Liberty*
John Stuart Mill's *Utilitarianism*
Hans Morgenthau's *Politics Among Nations*
Thomas Paine's *Common Sense*
Thomas Paine's *Rights of Man*
Thomas Piketty's *Capital in the Twenty-First Century*
Robert D. Putman's *Bowling Alone*
John Rawls's *Theory of Justice*
Jean-Jacques Rousseau's *The Social Contract*
Theda Skocpol's *States and Social Revolutions*
Adam Smith's *The Wealth of Nations*
Sun Tzu's *The Art of War*
Henry David Thoreau's *Civil Disobedience*
Thucydides's *The History of the Peloponnesian War*
Kenneth Waltz's *Theory of International Politics*
Max Weber's *Politics as a Vocation*
Odd Arne Westad's *The Global Cold War: Third World Interventions And The Making Of Our Times*

POSTCOLONIAL STUDIES

Roland Barthes's *Mythologies*
Frantz Fanon's *Black Skin, White Masks*
Homi K. Bhabha's *The Location of Culture*
Gustavo Gutiérrez's *A Theology of Liberation*
Edward Said's *Orientalism*
Gayatri Chakravorty Spivak's *Can the Subaltern Speak?*

The Macat Library By Discipline

PSYCHOLOGY

Gordon Allport's *The Nature of Prejudice*
Alan Baddeley & Graham Hitch's *Aggression: A Social Learning Analysis*
Albert Bandura's *Aggression: A Social Learning Analysis*
Leon Festinger's *A Theory of Cognitive Dissonance*
Sigmund Freud's *The Interpretation of Dreams*
Betty Friedan's *The Feminine Mystique*
Michael R. Gottfredson & Travis Hirschi's *A General Theory of Crime*
Eric Hoffer's *The True Believer: Thoughts on the Nature of Mass Movements*
William James's *Principles of Psychology*
Elizabeth Loftus's *Eyewitness Testimony*
A. H. Maslow's *A Theory of Human Motivation*
Stanley Milgram's *Obedience to Authority*
Steven Pinker's *The Better Angels of Our Nature*
Oliver Sacks's *The Man Who Mistook His Wife For a Hat*
Richard Thaler & Cass Sunstein's *Nudge: Improving Decisions About Health, Wealth and Happiness*
Amos Tversky's *Judgment under Uncertainty: Heuristics and Biases*
Philip Zimbardo's *The Lucifer Effect*

SCIENCE

Rachel Carson's *Silent Spring*
William Cronon's *Nature's Metropolis: Chicago And The Great West*
Alfred W. Crosby's *The Columbian Exchange*
Charles Darwin's *On the Origin of Species*
Richard Dawkin's *The Selfish Gene*
Thomas Kuhn's *The Structure of Scientific Revolutions*
Geoffrey Parker's *Global Crisis: War, Climate Change and Catastrophe in the Seventeenth Century*
Mathis Wackernagel & William Rees's *Our Ecological Footprint*

SOCIOLOGY

Michelle Alexander's *The New Jim Crow: Mass Incarceration in the Age of Colorblindness*
Gordon Allport's *The Nature of Prejudice*
Albert Bandura's *Aggression: A Social Learning Analysis*
Hanna Batatu's *The Old Social Classes And The Revolutionary Movements Of Iraq*
Ha-Joon Chang's *Kicking Away the Ladder*
W. E. B. Du Bois's *The Souls of Black Folk*
Émile Durkheim's *On Suicide*
Frantz Fanon's *Black Skin, White Masks*
Frantz Fanon's *The Wretched of the Earth*
Eric Foner's *Reconstruction: America's Unfinished Revolution, 1863-1877*
Eugene Genovese's *Roll, Jordan, Roll: The World the Slaves Made*
Jack Goldstone's *Revolution and Rebellion in the Early Modern World*
Antonio Gramsci's *The Prison Notebooks*
Richard Herrnstein & Charles A Murray's *The Bell Curve: Intelligence and Class Structure in American Life*
Eric Hoffer's *The True Believer: Thoughts on the Nature of Mass Movements*
Jane Jacobs's *The Death and Life of Great American Cities*
Robert Lucas's *Why Doesn't Capital Flow from Rich to Poor Countries?*
Jay Macleod's *Ain't No Makin' It: Aspirations and Attainment in a Low Income Neighborhood*
Elaine May's *Homeward Bound: American Families in the Cold War Era*
Douglas McGregor's *The Human Side of Enterprise*
C. Wright Mills's *The Sociological Imagination*

Thomas Piketty's *Capital in the Twenty-First Century*
Robert D. Putman's *Bowling Alone*
David Riesman's *The Lonely Crowd: A Study of the Changing American Character*
Edward Said's *Orientalism*
Joan Wallach Scott's *Gender and the Politics of History*
Theda Skocpol's *States and Social Revolutions*
Max Weber's *The Protestant Ethic and the Spirit of Capitalism*

THEOLOGY

Augustine's *Confessions*
Benedict's *Rule of St Benedict*
Gustavo Gutiérrez's *A Theology of Liberation*
Carole Hillenbrand's *The Crusades: Islamic Perspectives*
David Hume's *Dialogues Concerning Natural Religion*
Immanuel Kant's *Religion within the Boundaries of Mere Reason*
Ernst Kantorowicz's *The King's Two Bodies: A Study in Medieval Political Theology*
Søren Kierkegaard's *The Sickness Unto Death*
C. S. Lewis's *The Abolition of Man*
Saba Mahmood's *The Politics of Piety: The Islamic Revival and the Feminist Subject*
Baruch Spinoza's *Ethics*
Keith Thomas's *Religion and the Decline of Magic*

COMING SOON

Chris Argyris's *The Individual and the Organisation*
Seyla Benhabib's *The Rights of Others*
Walter Benjamin's *The Work Of Art in the Age of Mechanical Reproduction*
John Berger's *Ways of Seeing*
Pierre Bourdieu's *Outline of a Theory of Practice*
Mary Douglas's *Purity and Danger*
Roland Dworkin's *Taking Rights Seriously*
James G. March's *Exploration and Exploitation in Organisational Learning*
Ikujiro Nonaka's *A Dynamic Theory of Organizational Knowledge Creation*
Griselda Pollock's *Vision and Difference*
Amartya Sen's *Inequality Re-Examined*
Susan Sontag's *On Photography*
Yasser Tabbaa's *The Transformation of Islamic Art*
Ludwig von Mises's *Theory of Money and Credit*

Printed in the United States
by Baker & Taylor Publisher Services